Mrs. R̶̶

COLONIAL DAYS AND DAMES

GUNSTON HALL, VIRGINIA

Built about 1729.

COLONIAL
DAYS & DAMES

BY

Anne Hollingsworth Wharton

With Illustrations by E.S. Holloway

BENJAMIN BLOM, INC.
Publishers, New York 1971

First published Philadelphia, 1895
Reissued 1971 by
Benjamin Blom, Inc.
New York, N.Y. 10025

Library of Congress
Catalog Card Number 77-173127

TO THE MEMORY OF AN HONORED COLONIAL
DAME OF TO-DAY,

DEBORAH BROWN COLEMAN,

THIS BRIEF RECORD OF
COLONIAL LIFE

IS

Affectionately Dedicated.

1*

at Chalkley Hall

PREFACE.

WHILE men still recall the rustic pleasures of an old country seat in New York whose site is now the heart of the great metropolis, or remember forest trees surrounding a house at the corner of Twelfth and Chestnut Streets in Philadelphia, or tell of a boyhood spent in the pretty country town of Boston where stagecoaches clattered in from the rural districts, it seems time to collect in permanent form memorials of a past that cannot much longer be held in the memory of the living. By talking with men and women who lived in the first quarter of this century, we not only learn how our great cities appeared before the advent of the railroad, the steamboat, and the telegraph, but also, reaching back through their family traditions, are placed in touch with the scenes of the Revolution and, even further back, with those of Colonial days.

To give glimpses of social and domestic life North and South, gathered from such recollections and from diaries and letters, rather than to present a full or connected story of Colonial times, have these pages been written. For manuscripts, pictures, and data placed at my disposal, I take pleasure in making grateful acknowledgment to Mr. Justin Winsor, of Cambridge, to General Loring and Mr. Henry Ernest Woods, of Boston, to Mr. Matthew Clarkson, of New York, to Miss Adelaide L. Fries, of Salem, North Carolina, and to Dr. Charles J. Stillé, Mr. David Lewis, Mr. Edward Shippen, Dr. Charles Cadwalader, Mr. F. J. Dreer, Mrs. Oliver Hopkinson, and Miss Marion Wetherill, of Philadelphia.

A. H. W.

November, 1894.

CONTENTS.

9

COLONIAL DAYS.

"I SHALL call that my country where
I may most glorify God and enjoy the
presence of my dearest friends," wrote
Governor Winthrop from Massachusetts
to his absent wife; while the Rev. Francis
Higginson, stronger in his expressions of
renunciation for himself and others, has
left the following testimony in his diary:
"When we are in our graves, it will be
all one whether we have lived in plenty
or penury, whether we have dyed in a
bed of downe or lockes of straw. Onely

this is the advantage of the meane con-
dition, that it is a more freedom to dye.
And the lesse comfort any have in the
things of this world, the more liberty they
have to lay up treasure in heaven."

Although many of the Colonists came
to the shores of the New World with such
words upon their lips, and, we may believe,
with such sentiments in their minds, it was
not long before sturdy Anglo-Saxon enterprise and English love of home comfort
led them to make the wilderness, if not to
blossom like the rose of the Scriptures, at
least to take upon it something approach-
ing civilization.

No stronger contrast is to be found in
Colonial history than the sad story of the
earliest Virginia settlements, wiped out one
after the other by starvation and the hos-
tility of the natives, with that of the Massachusetts Colonists, clinging with English
tenacity to their rock-bound coast, defying
danger, cold, and hunger, guarding their
scant stores, restraining their appetites,—
planting the first corn that fell in their
way, showing their wisdom in that dark

day by providing for a still darker one,—watchful, alert, devout, trusting in the protection of an unseen Father, a body of deeply religious men and women, even if in the exercise of their faith they were often harder than the stones with which they ground their corn.

The expressions of the New England settlers often seem to us too spiritual to be natural in an hour when temporal needs pressed sorely upon them, yet the promise which they claimed for themselves—" Seek ye first the kingdom of God, and his righteousness; and all these things shall be added unto you"—was destined to be fulfilled, if not to them, to their children in the next generation, in greater comfort of living, in peace and prosperity, in manufactures and commerce. Dwelling-, meeting-, and school-houses sprang up all over the eastern portion of the Colony, and sixteen years after the little company of Pilgrims had coasted along the shores of Massachusetts, in terror of starvation, of cold, and of the Indians, a college was founded. A humble enough structure was

the first building raised at Harvard, although there were those who pronounced
it "too gorgeous for the wilderness."

In glancing over the Colonies, North and
South, there seems to have been no life
more delightful than that of Maryland and
Virginia.   Handsome, spacious mansions,
a fertile soil, genial climate, fine horses,
and retinues of servants conspired to give
the home life of the Southern planter many
of the characteristics of English country
living.   Yet with all its advantages a discouraging record is that of the first efforts
to colonize Virginia.   John Quincy Adams
said, in an oration delivered early in this
century, that the final success of the Virginia
settlements was largely due to the example
of Massachusetts.   As these settlements
were started long before that of Plymouth,
and as the places of those who failed were
speedily filled by others, ready and willing
to try the hazardous experiment, it seems
as if the ultimate triumph of Virginia colonization might be fairly attributed to the
courage and perseverance of the settlers
themselves.   When men equal to the un-

dertaking were sent over, the settlement
. of the Colony became an assured success,
despite pestilence, starvation, and the constant harrying of the borders by hostile
Indians.   Governor Dudley's pathetic letter to the Countess of Lincoln, written
soon after he came to Salem, finds a par-
allel in the expressions of Lord Delaware,
who says that if the " much cold comfort,"
in the way of bad news of the settlements,
that met him upon his arrival in 1610 had
not been accompanied by tidings of the
coming over of Sir Thomas Gates, " it
had binne sufficient to have broke my
heart."

The story of rude beginnings and established prosperity is substantially the same
all along the coast.   In Pennsylvania, New
Jersey, and Delaware, fair and judicious
dealings with the Indians insured peace
between them and the settlers for many
years.   We read of a Mrs. Chandler, " who
came to Philadelphia at the first landing,
having lost her husband on shipboard
[probably from small-pox], and who was
left with eight or nine children.   Her com-

panions prepared her the usual settlement
in a cave on the river-bank. So great was
the sympathy felt for this lady that even
the Indians brought her supplies and gifts,
and later a Friend [meaning a Quaker]
built a house and gave her a share of it."
Yet how few complaints we find! how simply the record reads! The chronicler of the
time dwells more upon the climate, pro-
ductions of the country, characteristics of
the natives, and improvements made up to
1696, which included "several good schools
for the teaching of youth," than upon the
struggles and privations of the settlers. So
much was this the case, that of the early
voyages to Pennsylvania, when small-pox
often ravaged the ship's company, we
find almost no detailed account. Sometimes the fact is mentioned in a letter to a
friend, as when James Claypoole writes to
Robert Turner that he hears that thirty-
one persons have died of small-pox in
William Penn's ship, the Welcome. There
were only one hundred passengers in all.
Elsewhere, Townsend and Story tell us
that the Proprietary himself assisted good

Dr. Thomas Wynne in the care of the sick and dying.

As an illustration of the primitiveness of this early living, we find the following story of little Rebecca Coleman, who came over with the first Pennsylvania settlers. At the door of her cave, when one day sitting there eating her milk porridge, she was heard to say again and again, " Now thee shan't," and again, " Keep to thy part." Upon investigation it was discovered that the child's " thees" and " thous" were addressed to a snake with which, in the most confiding manner, and with strict regard to justice, she was sharing her supper of milk porridge from a bowl placed upon the ground. " Happy simplicity and peacefulness !" adds the chronicler, for these were days when no tale was complete without its moral, " reminding one strongly of the Bible promise, when the weaned child should put its hand on the cockatrice's den." The promise was literally fulfilled in the case of little Rebecca Coleman, as she suffered no injury, and, having survived the perils of the early settlement, lived

to within a few years of the Revolution.
Great changes was she destined to witness
in her life of ninety-two years! Philadelphia, then a high river-bank, with a dense
forest back of it, was soon to be what
Gabriel Thomas found it, a "noble and
beautiful city," containing "a number of
houses, all inhabited, and most of them
stately and of brick, generally three stories
high, after the mode of London." This in
1696, while in 1744, William Black wrote
that Philadelphia far exceeded all descriptions he had heard of it. He was specially
impressed by the number of privateers in
the harbor, "the Considerable Traffick, in
shipping and unshipping of Goods, mostly
American Produce," and the comfort and
even luxury in which dwelt Mr. Andrew
Hamilton, Secretary Peters, Mr. Thomas
Lawrence, and others who entertained
him.

Mr. Black grows quite enthusiastic over
the markets of Philadelphia, from which,
he says, "You may be Supply'd with every
Necessary for the Support of Life thro'ut
the whole year, both Extraordinary Good

and reasonably Cheap, and it is allow'd by
Foreigners to be the best of its bigness in
the known World, and undoubtedly the
largest in America; I got to the place by
7; and had no small satisfaction in seeing
the pretty Creatures, the Young Ladies,
traversing the place from Stall to Stall,
where they could make the best Market,
some with their Maid behind them with a
Basket to carry home the Purchase, Others
that were designed to buy but trifles, as a
little fresh Butter, a Dish of Green Peas, or
the like, had Good Nature and Humility
enough to be their own Porter." This pleasing picture, even after making some allowance for the floridness of Mr. Black's style,
suggests comfort and plenty sufficient to
present a strong contrast to the minds of
those who, like Rebecca Coleman, were
able to recall the hardships of the first settlement of Pennsylvania; while in New
England the "city-like town of Boston
with its beautiful and large buildings," described by a traveller in 1649, marked rapid
progress from the little companies at Salem
and Charlestown drawing close together

for safety upon the three hills of Shaw-
mut.

The strongest reason for the final triumph over many and great obstacles in the
early settlement is doubtless to be found
in the character of the immigrants.   Mr.
Hollister, in his " History of Connecticut,"
after stating that many of those who came
to New England were from the humbler
walks of life, says, " The planters, the substantial landholders, who began to plant
those ' three vines in the wilderness,' sprung
from the better classes, and a large proportion of them from the landed gentry of
England.   This fact is proved not only by
tracing individual families, but by the very
names that those founders of our republic
bore."

True as this was of New England,
with its Winthrops, Saltonstalls, Endi-
cotts, Winslows, Bradfords, Pynchons, and
Wentworths, it was equally the case in the
Middle and Southern Colonies, to which
early came the Livingstons, Schuylers,
Crugers, De Peysters, De Lanceys, Montgomerys, Peningtons, Lloyds, Rodneys,

Calverts, Francises, Ravenels, Pringles, and Izards. If, as has often been said, and with some truth, Virginia was a Botany Bay for English criminals, it is only fair to acknowledge that many of these were political offenders, and as likely to be in the right as their accusers. England also sent to this Colony the Washingtons, Fairfaxes, Byrds, Harrisons, Spotswoods, Culpepers, Skipwiths, Pages, and Randolphs.

One needs only to glance over these names to realize that they did not, as a rule, belong to irresponsible adventurers, although of such there were some in all the Colonies.

Men who came from families of good position on the other side of the water felt it no dishonor to put their hands to any honest toil that had for its object the work of home-making and nation-building. Hence among the first settlers of Pennsylvania we find many good English names connected with the trades of tailor, hatter, carpenter, and the like, while from early New England records we learn

that Roger Wolcott, a Colonial governor
and a man of letters, worked in the field;
that Governor Leete kept a store; while
John Dunton, when he came to Boston in
1696, rejoiced to find Mr. Samuel Shrimp-
ton's "stately house there, with a Brass
Kettle atop, to show his Father was not
ashamed of his Original."

Later, when the idea of good livings to
be made in a country where land was to
be had for the asking and where fortunes
might be gained through trade with the
Indies, prevailed through Great Britain and
the Continent, a different class of people
came to America.   Many of these were
skilled workers, thrifty in their habits,
good, law-abiding citizens, like the Scotch
and Irish from Ulster and the Germans
who settled Germantown and came in
such numbers to other portions of Pennsylvania.

In the Southern Colonies there seem to
have been fewer men of a practical stamp
in the earliest immigrations; hence from
Virginia, John Smith, and later Lord Delaware, wrote home that they could not set-

tle the Colony without " men of quality, and painstaking men of arts and practices, chosen out and sent into the business." This was William Penn's principle, so strongly emphasized in the settlement of Pennsylvania, that the learning of a trade was the fittest equipment for colonization. Mr. Douglas Campbell has recounted the debt that the New England settlers owe to their temporary residence among the thrifty Hollanders, in legislation as well as in manufactures, commerce, and other arts of life. Pennsylvania also owes something to the Dutch, as it is safe to believe that the founder of the Province derived many of the practical elements in his well-balanced character from his Dutch mother, Margaret Jasper.

Simplicity of manners prevailed for many years from necessity, but the settlers of Pennsylvania surrounded themselves with whatever comforts and conveniences they could command. An extensive commerce was soon established with the Indies and the ports of Southern Europe, while the Germans and the Scotch - Irish added much to the industrial prosperity of the Province.*

Substantial and convenient houses were soon built, among these Robert Turner's "great and famous house," so often spoken of, and the Proprietary's house in Letitia Court, for which, as well as for the construction of his "Pennsbury Palace," the finer part of the framework was sent over from England. The ancient doorway of the latter house bore the cheerful and inviting ornament of a vine and cluster of grapes.

The first Edward Shippen is said to have "surpassed his contemporaries in the style and grandeur of his edifice and appurtenances for crossing the water," which latter phrase, we conclude, refers to boats used for business or pleasure, as Mr. Shippen's grounds extended to Dock Creek. This

---

* German linen, camlets, and serges were made in Germantown as early as 1696, and Judge Samuel W. Pennypacker says that to the Germans is due the honor of establishing the first paper-mill in America, in 1690, and of printing the Bible in their own tongue nearly forty years before it was printed in English.

house on South Second Street, afterwards
called the Governor's House, had an or-
chard and fine garden around it, which,
says the admiring chronicler, "equalizes
any I have ever seen, having a very famous
and pleasant summer-house erected in the
middle of his garden, abounding with
tulips, pinks, carnations, roses and lilies,
not to mention those that grew wild in the
fields, and also a fine lawn upon which
reposed his herd of tranquil deer."

If the Friend modestly, or with an affec-
tation of modesty, called his coach "a con-
venience," it was none the less a coach.
The Proprietary early drove his coach in
Philadelphia, and from thence to Pennsbury, and Isaac Norris, the son of an English merchant who had settled in Jamaica,
sent to England for a coach, and, although
a strict Quaker, did not scruple to have
the three falcons' heads of the family shield
emblazoned upon its side. The Norrises
also had their portraits painted while
in London, which was a custom objected
to later by Quakers as savoring of the
world. In her picture by Kneller, Mrs.

B   3

Isaac Norris appears as one of the most beautiful women of her time, nor is her costume strictly Friendly, the prevailing colors being red and green, the lovely hair rolled back from the forehead and worn without a cap.

There was no persecution for religion in Pennsylvania; but there was less friendliness between the Quakers and the Church people, as the latter came to have more authority and influence in the government. Such spicy expletives as the " Hot Church Party," and "Colonel Quarry's Packed Vestry," we find in the mouths of good Friends of the day, while William Penn, in a letter to James Logan, says that Governor Gookin has presented Parson Evans* with "two as gaudy and costly Common Prayer Books as the Queen has in her chapel, and intends as fine a Communion table, both of which charm the baby in the Bishop of London, as well as Parson Evans."

---

* This was the Rev. Evan Evans, rector of Christ Church parish in 1719.

Something like uniformity of thought and purpose prevailed in Colonial New England, with the exception of Rhode Island, which, like the Provinces of Pennsylvania and Maryland, early became a refuge for the disaffected from the neighboring settlements, naturally inducing a more restless religious life and a larger religious toleration. Mr. Lodge attributes the strong and sustained individuality of the New England people not simply to their Puritanism, but also to the fact that they were of English strain, with only slight admixture from other nationalities. " Race, language, religious belief, manners, customs, and habits of mind and thought were," he says, " the same from the forests of Maine to the shores of Long Island Sound. . . . They were all pure Englishmen, the purest part of the race perhaps, for, during a century and a half [in 1765] they had lived in a New World, and received no fresh infusion of blood from any race but their own."

The Quaker who came to Pennsylvania was quite as single-minded as the Puritan

of New England, and as sincere and earnest
in following the guidance of that "inner
light" which stood with him for duty, conscience, all that belongs to the moral and
spiritual development of man, as was his
New England brother in carrying out the
rules and ordinances of the religious body
to which he belonged. While the New
England Colonies were developing along
their own lines, with scant charity for those
whose ideas ran in other channels, Pennsylvania, from her position and charter,
became the home not only of the English
and the Welsh Quaker, who came to it as
to his birthright of freedom, religious and
civil, but of the English Churchman, with
his more conservative notions; of the
Scotch-Irish Presbyterian, as firmly established in his spiritual convictions as the
Puritan, although less favorably placed by
Providence for the direction of his neighbor's conscience; of the Roman Catholic;
of the German and Swedish Lutheran;
and of many less distinct subdivisions of
Protestantism. Fourteen years after the
settlement of Pennsylvania, Gabriel Thomas

speaks of numerous places of worship in Philadelphia, — of one Anabaptist, one Swedish Lutheran, one Presbyterian, two Quaker meeting-houses, and of a fine church belonging to the Church of England people. This was Christ Church, built in 1695, before the English communion had found an abiding-place in the much older city of Boston. "The place is free for all persuasions," he adds, "in a sober and civil way; for the Church of England and the Quakers bear equal share in the government. They live friendly well together; there is no persecution for religion, nor ever like to be."

From the various admixture of nationalities and creeds in Pennsylvania was evolved, in less than a century, a population representing many shades of belief, political and religious, and with strongly marked differences in character and ways of living. The early Quakers seem to have been less rigid in their manners and customs than those who followed them. The simplicity in dress which gradually obtained was at first a protest against

3*

changes of fashion rather than to establish a garb that distinguished them from the world's people.

On his first landing in Pennsylvania, William Penn was habited in the Cavalier costume of the day, the gold bullion upon the coat being left off and the broad-brimmed hat worn without feathers. There were lace ruffles at the wrist, however, and some historians place a blue silk sash around the stalwart proportions of the Proprietary and a light dress sword by his side. A handsome, well-built man of thirty-eight was Penn at this time, with courtly, gracious manners, skilled in all manly exercises. With this picture in our minds, it is not difficult to believe the story handed down by Mrs. Preston, of the athletic Englishman entering into their games with the friendly Indians, and excelling them all in feats of agility, or that other tale about John Ladd. "Friend John, thou art Ladd by name, and a Ladd in comprehension!" exclaimed the Proprietary, when John Ladd signified his preference for ready money rather than for lots in payment for his ser-

vices in laying out the new city of Philadelphia, adding, " Dost thou not know this
will become a great city ?"

The proscriptions and admonitions that
came later from leading Friends at home
and " visiting Friends" from abroad were
issued in consequence of the large influx
into Pennsylvania of persons of other ways
of living and thinking, who brought with
them temptations for the younger portion
of the community, in dress, manners, and
habits. This dangerous contagion from
proximity to the world's people led the
women Friends of Burlington, New Jersey,
to issue a letter from their Yearly Meeting,
in 1726, in which they besought their sisters to beware of " divers undue Liberties
that are too frequently taken by some that
walk among us and are accounted of us,"
adding,—

"We are willing in the pure love of Truth which
hath mercifully visited our souls Tenderly to caution
and advise our Friends against those things we think
inconsistent with our Ancient Christian Testimony of
plainness in Apparel. Some of which we think proper
to particularize,—As first that immodest fashion of
hooped Petticoats or the imitation of them either by

something put into their petticoats to make them sit
full or wearing more than is necessary or any other
imitation whatsoever which we take to be but a Branch
springing from the same corrupt root of Pride.   And
also that none of our Friends accustom themselves to
wear their Gowns with superfluous folds behind but
plain and decent, nor to go without Aprons nor to wear
superfluous Gathers or Pleats in their Caps or Pinners.
Nor to wear their Heads dressed high behind, neither
to cut or lay their hair on their Foreheads or Temples.
And that Friends are careful to avoid wearing striped
shoes."

That Friendly warnings and preachings
against foolish fashions were not without
effect we learn from a letter written by
Thomas Chalkley to his wife from Tortola,
in the West Indies, whither he went in
1741 upon a visitation :*

"I have a little more which I cant well omit and
this is for those who wear hoops among us the Gover-
nours wife her two Sisters Capt hunts wife & the
young woman whose father turnd her out of Doors
wore hoops before they were Convinced of ye principles
of our friends being throughly Convinced ye Could

---

* Thomas Chalkley owned a large tract of land near
Frankford.   Here he lived, and on this property his
son-in-law, Abel James, built a handsome and substantial house, which he called Chalkley Hall.

were [they could wear] ym no longer and Divers fine young people have Left ym of Since they have ye Same Excuses hear [here] all ye year as our girls has in Summer. The Grate Lord of all gird our youth with the Girdle of truth and then they will not need those monstrous preposterous girdes of hoops I call it monstrous because if almighty God should make a woman in the same Shape her hoop makes her Everybody would Say truly So according to this real truth they make themselves Monsters by art."

Thrift and enterprise early insured a certain amount of substantial comfort among the settlers, while the great advantages offered by fine harbors all along the coast and the various marketable products of the country soon enabled them to build up an extensive trade with the East and West Indies, Spain, Portugal, and other countries. Foreign luxuries thus found their way to the Colonies, adding much to the pleasures of life, and seaport towns gained a wider outlook into the world beyond through the tales of adventure brought home by their sailor sons, such tales as Eleanor Putnam describes the Salem children enjoying upon evenings when "My Cousin the Captain" and his

c

old friend sailed again the voyages of their youth, disputing and agreeing again after the fashion of old-time cronies.

The most notable instance of a fortune made upon the seas is that of the Pepperell family.   The first William Pepperell came from Tavistock, England, to the Isle of Shoals, where he and his partner, Mr. Gibbons, sent out their fishing smacks on the shores, and later set up an establishment on one of the islands for the curing and sale of their fish.   On a visit to Kittery Point, Pepperell made the acquaintance of John Bray, from Plymouth, whose seventeen-year-old daughter, Margery, he fell in love with and married, a successful venture on the part of the suitor having given Mr. Bray sufficient confidence in him to be willing to accept him as a son-in-law.   Mr. Bray gave his daughter a tract of land upon the Point, where William Pepperell built a house, which was considerably added to by his son, Sir William Pepperell.   From this small beginning, in a little more than half a century, the largest fortune in New England was accumulated.   The Pepperells built vessels and sent many to the West Indies laden with lumber, fish, oil, and live-stock, to be exchanged for dry goods, wine, and salt, or to sell both vessel and cargo. Their largest business was in fisheries, however, and they are known to have had as many as a hundred small vessels on the Grand Banks at one time.

While the Southern Colony of Virginia had her great planters who, like " King Carter," were renowned for the sumptuousness and state in which they lived, New York could boast her famous Dutch traders who lived in substantial comfort in their "*Bouweries*" upon the outskirts of New Amsterdam, and Massachusetts could claim such successful merchants as Elias Hasket Derby, the eccentric Timothy Dexter, and " King Hooper," whose stately home, later known as the Collins and the Peabody House, from subsequent possessors, is still standing. Robert Hooper, Esq., of Marblehead, who built his house at Danvers, once Salem village, was something of a Tory, and when General Gage found Boston too hot for him, he removed to Danvers and took up his abode in the Hooper House, where he resided for several months, protected by two companies of troops which were encamped in its vicinity.

Madam Knight, in her famous journey on horseback through the country that stretches between Boston and New York, doubtless gives a faithful picture of the rough and uncomfortable living of that early time; this, however, was country living, and even then presented a great contrast to the life in villages and towns. She records of the Indians whom she meets, that they are "the most salvage of all the salvages of that kind that I had ever seen," yet they do not appear to have molested her, and if her entertainment was so hard at one "Ordinary" that she walked out, having paid, as she remarked, her sixpence for "the smell of her Dinner," and at another time objected to "the Pumpkin and Indian mixt Bred, and the Bare Legged Punch," and at Norwalk to her bed of corn husks, which, "when scratched up by Little Miss, Russelled as if she'd been in the

Barn amongst the Husks," there were other
places, as Saxton's at Stonington, the widow
Prentice's at New London, New Haven,
and Fairfield, where she was "well ac-
commodated as to victuals and Lodging,"
and hospitable entertainment was offered
her in the homes of the Rev. Gurden Saltonstall, of New London, and Governor
John Winthrop, of New Haven.

One of the most amusing passages of
Madam Knight's diary, and one that best
illustrates the crudity of the life of the time
and place, as well as her own native wit, is
the account of her experience at " Haven's
Tavern in the Narragansett Country,"
where, having retired to her room, which
was parted from the kitchen by a single
board partition, and "to a bed which tho
pretty hard, was yet neet and handsome,"
she finds herself unable to sleep because
of a dispute of some topers in the next
room over the signification of the name of
their country, Narragansett:

"One said it was named so by yᵉ Indians, because
there grew a Brier there, of a prodigious Highth and
bigness, the like hardly ever known, called by the

4

Indians Narragansett; And quotes an Indian of so
Barberous a name for his Author, that I could not
write it. His Antagonist Replyed no—It was from a
Spring it had its name, wch hee well knew where it was,
which was extreem cold in summer, and as Hott as
could be imagined in the winter, which was much
resorted too by the natives, and by them called Narragansett, (Hott and Cold,) and that was the originall of
their places name—with a thousand Impertinances not
worth notice, wch He utter'd with such a Roreing voice
and Thundering blows with the fist of wickedness on
the Table, that it peirced my very head. I heartily
fretted, and wish't 'um tongue tyed; but with as little
succes as a freind of mine once, who was (as shee said)
kept a whole night awake. on a Jorny, by a country
Left, and a Sergent, Insigne and a Deacon, contriving
how to bring a triangle into a Square. They kept calling for tother Gill, wch while they were swallowing,
was some Intermission."

This draught having had the effect of
augmenting the turmoil, or, as she says,
"like Oyle to fire," increasing the flame,
the philosophical traveller set her candle
upon a chest and in the following lines
endeavored to turn the roisterers' own
weapons against them :

> " I ask thy Aid, O Potent Rum !
> To charm these wrangling Topers Dum.
> Thou hast their Giddy Brains possest—

The man confounded wth the Beast—
And I, poor I, can get no rest.
Intoxicate them with thy fumes:
O still their Tongues till morning comes.

" And I know not but my wishes took effect; for the dispute soon ended wth tother Dram; and so Good night!"

It is gratifying to learn that this heroic if " fearfull female traiveller" finally reached her destination, New York, where she was received by Mr. Thomas Burroughs, a prominent merchant of that place, who aided her in attending to the business for which she had made this perilous journey, and afterwards entertained her with such pleasing diversions as a ride to witness the sleighing between New York and the Bowery,* followed by " a handsome Entertainment of five or six dishes and choice Beer and metheglin Cyder," at the house of Madam Dowes, a gentlewoman who lived at a farm

---

* A small town on the banks of the Harlem River, which was a favorite resort of riding and sleighing parties of the time. The name Bowery was evidently derived from Governor Stuyvesant's *bouwery*, or farm, near by.—Valentine's History of the City of New York.

in the neighborhood. Of the sleighing Madam Knight says, " I believe we mett 50 or 60 slays that day—they fly with great swiftness and some are so furious that they'll turn out of the path for none except a London Cart."

Mr. Burroughs also took Madam Knight to a " Vendue," where she met with a great bargain in paper, and became acquainted with a number of persons, who invited her to their houses and generously entertained her. It was upon this journey that she met Madam Livingston, wife of Lieutenant-Colonel John Livingston, whose second wife was to be Mrs. Knight's own and only daughter, Elizabeth, at this time a girl of seventeen. Her impressions Madam Knight records, in a general way, as follows : " New York is a pleasant, well compacted place, situated on a commodious river which is a fine harbor for shipping, the Buildings, Brick Generaly, very stately and high, though not altogether like ours in Boston. . . ."

" They have Vendues very frequently and make their earnings very well by them, for they treat with good

Liquor Liberally, and the Customers Drink as Liberally and Generally pay for 't as well, by paying for that which they Bidd up Briskly for, after the sack has gone plentifully about, tho' sometimes good penny worths are got there."

Surely this good dame was not lacking in shrewdness, which, with her forcible use of the English tongue, even if in writing it she was sometimes guilty of such trifling errors as the misplacing of vowels and consonants, rendered her worthy of being the early preceptress of such distinguished men as Dr. Samuel Mather and Dr. Franklin, who both attended her Dame's school established in Boston after her return from this journey to New York. In another part of her journal she says of the New Yorkers, "Nor do they spare for any diversion the place affords, and sociable to a degree, they'r Tables being as free to their Naybours as to themselves."

"The English go very fasheonable in their dress. The Dutch, especially the middling sort, differ from our women, in their habitt go loose, were French muches wch are like a Capp and a head band in one, leaving their ears bare, which are sett out wth Jewells of a large size and many in number. And their fingers hoop't with Rings, some with large stones in them of many Coullers as were their pendants in their ears, which You should see very old women wear as well as Young."

Such were the life, customs, and dress of the mixed population of Dutch and English in New York in 1704, and we find equally strong contrasts occurring, a little later in Philadelphia, between the Quakers and the world's people. If the former appeared in sober attire, the gayer descendants of the early settlers arrayed themselves in long red cloaks, in an exaggerated style of dress called "trollopes," very objectionable to quiet folk, in hoops so large that the wearer was obliged to enter a door crab-like, "pointing her obtruding flanks end foremost," high-heeled shoes and stiff stays, which seem to have been worn by both sexes, as were the large curled wigs of the period. The very boys wore wigs, says Watson, and their dress in general resembled that of the men, which was quite as absurd in its way as the women's, including coat-skirts lined and stiffened with buckram, or set out with wadding like a coverlet, and sleeves with cuffs reaching to the elbows, with lead in them to keep them down.

What would Nathaniel Ward have had to say to men who thus bedecked their persons? He had already declared himself with regard to "women who lived to ape the latest fashion" in no measured terms, denominating the five or six such in the Colony of Massachusetts as "the very gizzard of a trifle, the product of a quarter of a cipher, the epitome of nothing," to which he added, "It is no marvel they wear trails on the hinder part of their heads, having nothing it seems in the forepart but a few squirrels' brains to help them frisk from one ill favored fashion to another." The fashions of both men and women, cited by Watson, were doubtless somewhat exaggerated in the transmission from one generation to another, and in a short time "long red cloak" and "trollopes" had to give way before offensive caricatures aimed at them, a female felon being led to the gallows in the former, while the wife of Daniel Pettiteau, the hangman, paraded the town in the latter.*

A curious notice from the *Pennsylvania Gazette* shows that certain feminine adornments, and even one of the much-derided red cloaks, had found their way into a household of such simplicity as the Franklins' as early as 1750.

" Whereas on Saturday night last, the house of Benjamin Franklin, of this city, printer, was broken open, and the following things feloniously taken away, viz. a double necklace of gold beads, a woman's long scarlet cloak, almost new, with a double cape, a woman's gown, of printed cotton, of the sort called brocade print, very remarkable, the ground dark, with large red roses, and other large and yellow flowers, with blue in some of the flowers, with many green leaves ; a pair of woman's stays, covered with white tabby before, and dove-colour'd tabby behind, with two large steel hooks, and sundry other goods.   Whoever discovers the thief, or thieves, either in this or any of the neighbouring provinces, so that they may be brought to justice, shall receive Ten Pounds reward ; and for recovering any of the goods, a reward in proportion to their value, paid by   BENJAMIN FRANKLIN."

It is evident that there was enough worldliness abroad in Philadelphia to lead

* Watson's Annals, vol. i. p. 184.

prominent Quakers to issue such letters as
that of the Women Friends of Burlington
and of Thomas Chalkley, especially as a
traveller of veracity has assured us that
young Quakeresses were fond of ribbons
and other gayeties in attire.

Watson found so many diversions to
record that he devotes a separate chapter to
"Sports and Amusements," in which he
tells of the "High Dutch" skating of Dr.
Foulke, the celebrated surgeon, and of "Ox
Roasts" on the thick-ribbed ice of the Delaware River, in the presence of numerous
skaters, the skaters of Philadelphia being
pre-eminent.

Mrs. Ball advertised her school for
teaching French, playing on the spinet, and
dancing, in Letitia Court, about 1730; and
a few years later, when, in consequence of
the religious fervor excited by the preaching of Whitefield, dancing-schools, concert-
rooms, and play-houses were closed, there
was strong opposition to such stringent
measures from a certain portion of the
community, some of the gentlemen even
breaking open the doors. The famous

Dancing Assembly, whose lists run down
to our own day, was established in 1749.
Places in the dance were arranged by lot,
and partners were engaged for the evening,
" leaving nothing," says the astute chronicler, " to the success of forwardness or
favouritism. Gentlemen always drank tea
with their partners the day after the assembly,—a sure means of producing a more
lasting acquaintance, if desirable." It is
to be hoped that pretty Quakeresses were
sometimes allowed to participate in the
milder festivity of such tea-drinkings, even
if the more exciting pleasures of the dance
were denied them.

If gayeties and luxuries rapidly increased
in Pennsylvania, it is gratifying to know
that churches, meeting-houses, and schools
kept pace with the one, and that the commerce and manufactures of a largely industrial population balanced and contributed to the demands of the other.

The first school in Philadelphia, opened
by Enoch Flower in 1683, was soon followed by a grammar-school, established
by Samuel Carpenter and other leading

Friends. Over this school, in which the "learned languages were taught," presided George Keith, a Scotch Friend, who later joined the English Church and became a grievous "thorn in the flesh" of good Quakers. Keith was assisted in his teaching by Thomas Makin, who occasionally indulged in flights of poetry; but, finding pedagogy more popular than poetry, he finally became principal of the grammar-school in Keith's place, and carried it on with fair success. It is a curious fact that the small and now almost unknown seaboard town of Lewes boasted so superior a school for girls that Governor Lloyd sent his daughters there to complete their education, while to a little settlement in Bucks County belongs the honor of opening the first institution for collegiate instruction in the Middle Colonies. The Log College, founded by the Rev. William Tennent in 1726, in which undertaking he was greatly assisted by his cousin James Logan, became the *alma mater* of such distinguished divines as William Tennent the younger, Samuel Finley, the Blairs,

Charles Beatty, and William Robinson, besides claiming the distinction of being the corner-stone of Princeton College, established more than twenty years later.

An anecdote is told of the Rev. Charles Beatty, an early graduate of the Log College, by Dr. Franklin, which admirably illustrates the ready mother wit of the latter.

Dr. Beatty was acting as chaplain to an army of five hundred men led by Franklin to defend the frontier against the French and Indians after the burning of the Moravian mission at Gnadenhütten, Pennsylvania.

"Dr. Beatty complained to me," says Franklin, "that the men did not generally attend his prayers and exhortations. When they were enlisted, they were promised, besides hay and provisions, a gill of rum a day, which was punctually served out to them, half in the morning, and the other half in the evening; and I observed they were as punctual in attending to receive it; upon which I said to Mr. Beatty, 'It is perhaps below the dignity of your profession to act as steward of the rum, but if *you* were to deal it out, and only just after prayers, you would have them all about you.'"

The shrewd suggestion was adopted by

Dr. Beatty, and the philosophic Franklin adds,—

> "Never were prayers more generally and more punctually attended; so that I thought this method preferable to the punishment inflicted by some military laws for non-attendance on divine service."

The fact that a Presbyterian minister would, under any circumstances, consent to measure out rum to his flock suggests a curious contrast between customs past and present; but, as each man received but half a gill at a time, the reverend gentleman may have considered that, in a certain sense, he was assisting in a temperance movement.

Thackeray has admirably hit off Dr. Franklin's readiness to advise upon all subjects in his picture of a dinner at Madam Esmond's, before the Braddock expedition, when General Braddock constantly turns to the " little Postmaster from Philadelphia" who seemed to possess much curious information and to have counsel to offer in all emergencies. Nothing seemed to be too great or too small for Franklin's

consideration.   While abroad upon diplo-
matic business, he writes his wife minute
directions about making and putting down
the carpets which he sends her; yet Mrs.
Franklin was herself a notable housekeeper.

In a letter written to her husband in
1765, she speaks of papered walls in their
new house in Franklin Court, while the
Fair Hill mansion boasted paper as early
as 1717, although the parlors were wains-
coted in oak and red cedar.   Several carpets Mrs. Franklin mentions as those in the
blue room, the parlor, and other rooms,
and even expresses a desire to have a
Turkey carpet, which sounds strangely
luxurious and modern to our ears, especially as the first carpet remembered in
Philadelphia was seen at the house of
Owen Jones, at Second and Spruce Streets,
about 1750.   These early carpets were not
very ample, being designed for the centre
of the room, the chairs being set around
the edges of the square, the middle of
which was occupied by the table.   Mrs.
Franklin also mentions such luxuries as

a closet with glass doors, spaces for the
" pier of glass," a harpsichord and harmon-
ica; while Sally's room, up two pairs of
stairs, beside its regular furniture, con-
tained a trunk and books which seem to
be quite beyond her powers of description,
as she adds, " but these you can't have any
notion of." Dr. Franklin, in one of his
earlier letters, speaks of such fancyings of
his own as a " pair of silk blankets, very
fine, just taken in a French prize," which
he thinks would be best to cover a summer
bed, some fine damask table-cloths and
napkins, snuffer-stand and extinguisher of
very beautiful workmanship, and some car-
peting " which is to be sewed together in
such a way as would make the figures
match, and to be finished with a border."

Carpets instead of sanded floors and
wall-paper in the place of the primitive
whitewash were finding their way into
modest households, while much greater
luxuries were to be seen in such resi-
dences as those of the Hamiltons, Allens,
Fishers, Morrises, Jameses, and Willings;
and, instead of the one maid-servant that

Gabriel Thomas speaks of in 1696 as
among the comforts of the early settlement, numbers of servants were to be
found in many households, some of them
slaves. The "slaves' gallery" is still to
be seen in old Christ Church in Boston,
and in Quaker Philadelphia some good
citizens owned slaves, and thought it no
harm to will a likely African or a neat-
handed yellow girl to their children, as
they left them their household furniture,
horses, and carriages. The days had
passed by, in 1760, when the carriages
and chariots driven in this city could be
told off on the fingers of two hands, as
in Mrs. Ilvaine's lines :

> " Judge Allen drove a coach and four
>   Of handsome dappled grays,
>   Shippens, Penns, Pembertons, and Morrises,
>   Powels, Cadwaladers, and Norrises
>   Drove only pairs of blacks and bays."

Du Simitière enumerates the carriages
driven in Philadelphia in 1772 as number-
ing nearly one hundred, although William
Peters and Thomas Willing could long

claim the distinction of driving the only landaus in old Philadelphia.

The time was long past, even in New England, when the iron hand of law or the voice of admonition could keep back the tide of progress in religious toleration or in the gentler arts of life. If, in early days in Plymouth, the settlers walked to the meeting, the governor and elders at their head, the men armed and equipped as for battle, the women, children, and servants well guarded from attack, the day came before the century was out when the governor rolled to the place of worship in his coach. In 1695, Judge Sewall writes that he prevailed upon "Governor Bradstreet and his Lady" * to walk to his new house and wish him joy of it, "after which they sat near an hour with Mrs. Corwin and Wharton, and the Governor drank a glass or two of wine, eat some fruit, and took a pipe of tobacco in the new Hall, and finally went away between twelve and one in Madame Richard's new Coach and horses."

---

* Simon Bradstreet's second wife, Mistress Gardner. His first wife, Anne, the poetess, died in 1672.

5*

Joseph Bennett, coming to New England somewhat later, writes, " There are several Familys in Boston that keep a Coach and pair of Horses, and some few drive with 4 horses; but for Chaises and Saddle Horses, considering the bulk of the place [they] out do London. When the Ladies ride out to take the Air it is generally in a Chaise or Chair; tho' but a single Horse'd one and they have a Negro servant to drive 'em."

The dancing of Morton and his followers at Merry Mount was promptly stopped and their scandalous May-pole cut down; yet there were others in New England who danced before the next century was old, as we find that Charles Bradstreet in 1739 was permitted by the selectmen of the town of Salem to " teach dancing" in connection with French, " so long as he keeps good order," while a little later Lawrence D'Obleville, a native of Paris and a Protestant, was employed in Salem and other towns " teaching children and youth to dance and good manners."

Although Governor Endicott cut the

cross out of the English flag because, to his mind, it savored of popery, it was restored to its place, and we find Samuel Sewall, fifty years later, still in doubt about this emblem in the colors, wondering whether it might not hinder his "Entrance into the Holy Land." Still greater and more grievous changes was he to behold whom Mr. Lodge signalizes as the "Last of the Puritans," when, under Governor Andros, the service of the English Church was permitted in Boston, and was heard within the walls of the venerated Old South. With the admission of the English Church, which meant an outward toleration for other religious bodies, there came into the very strongholds of Puritanism a wider liberty in manners, customs, and habits of life.

Tradition tells of a spirited Colonial lady, wife of a squire in Hadley, Massachusetts, who was formally excommunicated by the parson and elders of the meeting for the sin of being present at the Christmas celebration of two poor Germans living upon her husband's estate.

Slowly and steadily, however, the new wine was working in the old bottles, and although Samuel Sewall records with satisfaction, as late as Christmas, 1697, "Shops are open and Carts and Sleds come to Town with Wood and Fagots as formerly, save what abatement may be allowed on account of the wether," he is forced to conclude his characteristic entry with the discouraging statement that Joseph, his son, told him that "most of the Boys went to the Church," adding, "yet he went not." The old barriers were giving way, new customs and observances were coming in. In Puritan New England, as well as in Quaker Pennsylvania, the joyous holiday of Christian hope was being kept. In New Amsterdam the New-Year festival was a period of greater rejoicing, but in Virginia and the Southern Colonies an old-time English Christmas, with yule-log, mistletoe bough, and church services, early marked the season. In Pennsylvania there were many who held aloof from the observance of the day, but with less severity than the Puritan, the Quaker's inward light being apparently intended more for his own guidance than for that of his neighbor, and Watson speaks of May-Day and Christmas celebrations in Philadelphia as of long-established usage. Of the latter he records,—

"The 'Belsh Nichel' and St. Nicholas has been a time of Christmas amusement from time immemorial among us; brought in, it is supposed, among the sportive frolics of the Germans. It is the same also observed in New York, under the Dutch name of St. Claes. 'Belsh Nichel,' in high German, expresses 'Nicholas in his fur' or sheep-skin clothing. He is always supposed to bring good things at night to good children, and a rod for those who are bad."

The first signs of Christmas-keeping in New England seem to picture the dawn of a brighter day for the Puritan child, whose natural and spontaneous development must have been sadly checked and hampered by the straitness of the life surrounding it, even in homes where there was full and plenty, by the dismal Sabbaths which weighed heavily upon the exuberant energy of the healthy young creature, with their sermons of such length that Nathaniel Ward himself confesses, " we have a strong weakness

in New England that when we are speaking, we know not how to conclude, we make
many ends before we make an end."

In letters and diaries of the time we find
small mention of the children, except to
record their birth and death, or, perchance,
to note when they had the small-pox, or
when they were inoculated to prevent their
having it, as when Judge Lynde writes,—

"Daughter Lydia went to Boston, and was inoculated by Dr. Charles Pynchon; thro' God's goodness
had it so favourably as every day to be about, and in
14 days went out visiting, and on 5th May returned
well to Salem, Laus Deo!"

Sometimes an entry records the number
of olive-branches upon the family vine,
with a certain pride of possession, or tells
of some spiritual experience marking the
turning of the page from childhood to
manhood or womanhood. Scant space was
found in those days to dwell upon childish
joys, and when sorrows are mentioned they
seem strangely akin to those of the grown
folks, as when little Anne Dudley, at six or
seven, relates her grief, not over a fractured
doll or toy, but because of her "neglect of

Private Duteys" in which she is too often
tardy; while at sixteen, finding herself
" carnall and sitting loose from God," she
accepts the small-pox that then " smott"
her as a " proper rebuke to her pride and
vanity." Reared in such an atmosphere of
morbid conscientiousness and theological
disputation, the children in the streets
caught the current phrases, and during
the Hutchinson trial jeered one another
as believers in the " Covenant of Grace"
or in the " Covenant of Works." We
can only hope that certain pleasures in-
separable from country living belonged
to the children of New England. Even
the larger towns were but small settlements in those days, surrounded by
forests or bounded on one side or the
other by the sea. Hence we may believe
that the boys spent their recreation hours
in the woods or by the water, and that the
girls were sometimes permitted to leave
their tasks and stretch their limbs by entering into their brothers' sports,—fishing,
boating, nutting in the autumn woods, and,
rare diversion of the New England winter,

coasting down the long hills and skating upon the ponds!

Such pleasures being theirs, we may still rejoice that for Puritan children was coming, surely if slowly, the joy of the child's festival; and that all along the coast, from the scant observance in New England to the generous English celebration of the day in the Southern Colonies, the high festival of the Christian year was to bring expectancy, good cheer, well-filled stockings, gifts and greetings to the children who were destined to be the mothers and fathers of a great nation.

WOMEN IN THE EARLY SETTLE-MENT.

RUMORS have come to our ears of a toast to the Puritan Mothers, from those of their sons who meet together in the New England Society, to pour out libations, burn incense, and consume canvasback and terrapin in honor of their ancestors, the especial claim of these worthy dames upon the consideration of the present generation being based upon the fact that, in addition to enduring all the hardships that fell to the lot of the Puritan Fathers, they had to endure the Puritan Father himself. However this may have been, and we doubt not, with all due respect to

their sterling qualities, that some of these
progenitors of ours were, like Carlyle,
"gey ill to live wi'," it seems as if the
courage, patience, and heroism of the
pioneer women of America had not been
sufficiently honored.

Heroic and much-enduring women we
naturally think of in connection with the
Revolutionary struggle, but of such there
were not a few in the early settlement of
the country, whether upon the bleak hill-
sides of New England, where the winters
were more severe and the soil less produc-
tive than farther south, or upon the banks
of the Hudson and the Delaware, or still
farther south along the Chesapeake and the
James. A vision of the pioneer women
of the Massachusetts Colony, led by the
girlish figures of Mary Chilton and Priscilla Mullins, inevitably rises before the
retrospective student, because a certain
halo of romance has ever encircled these
two picturesque personalities.

Others there were, equally lovely and
quite as picturesque, whom the pens of the
romance writer and the poet have as yet

failed to touch. In the immigration to Salem in 1630 there came, in a vessel that bore her name, the Lady Arbella Johnson, daughter of the third Earl of Lincoln, in company with her husband, her sister Susan, wife of John Humphrey, the Dudleys, Simon Bradstreet and his "verse-making wife," the two daughters of Sir Robert Saltonstall, and other ladies of high degree who dined with the Lady Arbella in the "great cabin." Delicately nurtured and frail of constitution, Lady Arbella had been urged to remain in England for a time, but rather than be separated from her husband she was willing to brave the perils of the long voyage and the hardships of pioneer life in a strange land. She lived only to behold the shores of the new world clad in spring beauty, before closing her eyes forever to earthly visions, or, as Mr. Cotton Mather wrote years after, she "left an earthly *paradise* in the family of an Earldom, to encounter the sorrows of a *wilderness*, for the entertainments of a *pure worship* in the *house of God;* and then immediately left that *wilderness* for the Heavenly paradise." Of the husband of this lady, Mr. Isaac Johnson, who was one of the most influential men in the settlement, Mather wrote with quaint pathos,—

> " He try'd
> To live without her, lik'd it not, and dy'd.

His *mourning* for his amiable consort was too bitter to be extended a *year ;* about a month after *her* death *his* ensued, unto the extream loss of the whole plantation." Of how many more the same sad story could be told, we realize when we learn that of the small company that landed at Plymouth fifty died in two months, while the ranks of the settlers of Charlestown and Salem were sadly depleted by pestilence and starvation. The needs and distress of the colonists are plainly revealed by a picture, that has come down to us, of the first American Thanksgiving Day. A fast had been appointed, which it was not difficult to enforce, as the governor's last baking of bread had been put in the oven, and many of the settlers were subsist-

ing upon clams, acorns, and various nuts.
" 'Twas marvellous," says Mather, " to see
how *helpful* these good people were to one
another, following the example of their
most liberal governour Winthrop, who
made an equal distribution of what he
had in his own stores among the poor,
taking no thought of to-morrow."   It is
related that he was generously giving
from his own scant supply a handful of
meal to a poor man distressed by the wolf
at the door, when a ship was seen in the
harbor bearing provisions for all.   The fast
day was speedily turned into a season of
rejoicing, and the first formal proclamation
was issued for Thanksgiving Day by Governor Winthrop, who, in the face of all
discouragements, stoutly maintained that
if it were all to be done over again he
would do no differently.

The " contented mind" of the old adage
must have often provided those good people with a " continual feast," when there
was little else to serve, and we cannot but
admire the thankful spirit of a certain
" honest man who invited his friends to a

dish of clams, and at table offered up fervent thanks to Heaven who *had given* them to suck the abundance of the seas, and of the treasures hid in the sands."

Although there was less suffering from cold and hunger and far less mortality in the Provinces of Pennsylvania and New Jersey than in Massachusetts, there were many hardships and discomforts in settlements where few houses had been erected in advance. Many of the immigrants dwelt in caves along the banks of the Delaware, then a high, bold shore called Coaquannock. "These caves," says Watson, "were generally formed by digging into the ground, near the verge of the river-front bank, about three feet in depth; thus making half their chamber under ground; and the remaining half above ground was formed of sods of earth or earth and brush combined. The roofs were formed of layers of limbs, or split pieces of trees, over-laid with sod or bark, river rushes, etc. The chimneys were of stones and river pebbles, mortared together with clay and grass, or river reeds." This description answers to that of some of the Indian dwellings sufficiently to suggest that the friendly natives may have lent their new neighbors a hand in the preparation of these temporary abodes. The Owens' cave was on a shelving bank on the south side of Spruce Street west of Second, afterwards Townsend's Court. The Coateses, Morrises, Guests, and others dwelt in these primitive habitations until they were able to build themselves houses, the latter family living in a cave near the Crooked Billet wharf, so named from an old tavern on the river, north of Chestnut Street, which had a crooked billet of wood for its sign. From family papers we learn that when William and Elizabeth Hard arrived in Philadelphia the latter rejoiced and considered it an especial providence to find her sister, Alice Guest, whom she had not seen for years, living sumptuously in her own cave by the river bank, where Elizabeth and her husband were entertained. Of Mrs. Hard's own share in the building of her home, her niece, Deborah Morris, thus quaintly tells:

" All that came wanted a Dwelling and hastened to provide one. As they lovingly helped each other, the Women even set themselves to work that they had not been used to before ; for few of the first settlers were of the Laborous Class, and help of that source was scarce. My good Aunt thought it expedient to help her Husband at the end of the saw, and to fetch all such Water to make such kind of Mortar, as they then had to build their chimney. At one time being over-wearied therewith, her Husband desired her to forbear, saying, ' thou had better, my dear, think of dinner ;' on which, poor woman, she walked away, weeping as she went, reflecting on herself for coming here, to be exposed to such hardships, and then knew not where to get a dinner, for their Provision was all spent, except a small quantity of Biscuit and Cheese, of which she had not informed her Husband ; but thought she would try which of her friends had any to spare. Thus she walked on towards their tent (happy time when each one's treasure lay safe in their tents), but a little too desponding in her mind, for which she felt herself closely reproved, and as if queried with—' Did not thou come for liberty of conscience,—hast thou not got it, also been provided for beyond thy expectation ?' which so humbled her, she on her knees begged forgiveness and for Preservation in the near future and never Repined after.

" When she rose from her knees, and was going to seek for other food than what she had, her Cat came into the Tent, and had caught a fine large Rabbit, which she thankfully received and dressed as an English hare. When her Husband came to dinner, being informed of the particulars, they both wept with reverential Joy, and Eat their Meal, which was thus seasonably provided for them, in singleness of heart. Many such divinely Providential cares did they partake of. Thus did our worthy Witness the Arm of Divine love extended for Their Support within and without, which is not shorten'd, his love and Power remains the same and ever will to his depending Children."

It is interesting to know that relics of these Pennsylvania cave-dwellers have been preserved even to this century, one of the descendants of Mrs. Hard having, says Watson, "a very pretty chair, low and small, which had been a sitting-chair in that cave."

Still more pleasing is it to learn that comfort and prosperity fell to the share of Mr. and Mrs. Hard, and that when they and their Morris relatives owned family plate, some of it was marked with an engraved design of the faithful cat bearing in her mouth the providential rabbit.

Of John and Rebecca Head, who arrived in Philadelphia early in the last century, it is related that, having a flock of little ones to convey to their new home, and various household utensils, and there being no con-

veyance in those days, they hit upon the
expedient of putting the two younger girls
in a tub, each of the parents taking a handle.   The older children, Rebecca and
Mary, aged respectively four and three
years, walked in front, carrying all the
goods that their little hands could hold.
"Thus," says the narrator, Mr. George
Vaux, a descendant of one of these children, "our ancestors wended their way
from the water's edge to their first dwelling
place in the New World." [1]

Within half a century the Head family
became so prosperous that the descendants of the little children who took their
first American ride in a tub were able to
drive their carriages, one of them being
the ancestress of Johns Hopkins, whose
large fortune and generous spirit established in Baltimore the university and hospital that bear his name.   Another sister,
Esther, born in Philadelphia, was the an-

---

[1] This incident was related by one of these children,
Martha Head, to her grand-daughter, Philadelphia
Pemberton, who transmitted it to Mr. Vaux through his
cousin, Mary Ann Bacon.

cestress of the late George Sharswood, Chief Justice of the Supreme Court of Pennsylvania; while of another descendant, John Head, the following story is told. Robert Morris, the financier, was urged to apply to Mr. Head for assistance in the early days of the Revolution, when the Continental Congress was greatly hampered for money to provision and clothe the troops. Mr. Head was known to have made a large fortune in the shipping business, and, although he was a Quaker, it was hoped that he would yield to the entreaties of his friend Mr. Morris. The latter explained to the Quaker merchant the necessities of the case, the gloomy outlook for the winter, and the importance of raising a considerable sum of money for immediate use, to which Friend Head replied, after listening with much attention, " Thou knowest the principles of our society, and that I cannot conscientiously do anything to promote and keep up a war." Mr. Morris renewed his entreaties, with such effect that the old gentleman finally sprang up, saying,

" Robert, on that mantel is a key, in that room is an iron chest," and without another word upon the subject took up his hat and left the house.   A word to the wise was, in this instance, sufficient, as Mr. Morris took up the key and opened the chest, from which he took sixty thousand dollars in gold and silver, with which clothing, shoes, and other necessities were provided for the army.   Soon after, the battle of Trenton was fought, and the affairs of the Colonies assumed a brighter aspect.   The narrator adds that Mr. Morris left treasury notes to the amount of sixty thousand dollars in place of the coin, which notes were later redeemed by the new government, and the descendants of this patriotic and charitable Quaker are still enjoying the money which he was willing to risk *pro bono publico*.   Somewhat similar stories are told of Abel James, who, like John Head, was one of the wealthiest of the old Philadelphia merchants, and of John Morton.

There is no reason to doubt that these men all helped the Colonies in their hour of need, as they were men of large fortune, and like many other Friends, although opposed to war on general principles, considered the cause in which the Revolutionary party was engaged a just and righteous one.

Among others who came to Pennsylvania to endure the hardships of the early settlement, which were in some cases less to be dreaded than the persecution that beset them at home, were Robert Owen and his wife, from Wales. He had received a commission as Captain of the Militia and Governor of Beaumaris Castle, and, being unwilling to take an oath at the time of the Restoration, was imprisoned at Dolgelly, Merionethshire, for five years. To Robert Owen's wife, who was a sympathizing helpmeet in all his trials, one historian pays the following high tribute: "She was a woman rarely endowed with many natural gifts, and not given to many words."

Here also came Grace Thomas, whose son Gabriel wrote the first history of the Pennsylvania settlement, a small volume full of quaint observations and valuable

D   7

facts, and whose daughter Rachel was soon after her arrival married to the first Thomas Wharton, at the Bank Meeting-House on the Delaware, where so many couples were united. From the number of marriages early recorded, love-making seems to have been a favorite pastime upon those long voyages, which lasted more weeks than it now takes days to cross the Atlantic, especially when an unexpected trip to the West Indies was taken at the will of the wind. A certain Sea-mercy Adams, among the early arrivals, was married to Mary Brett; but the first Philadelphia bride was Priscilla Allen, who was married, in 1682, to Thomas Smith, they having passed one meeting in the Isle of Wight.

Many pioneer women who endured hardness for conscience' sake, and for the love of husbands and fathers, who brought them to these shores, were doubtless worth their weight in gold; but it is not recorded of all of them that this exact measure of appreciation was meted out to them as in the case of Sarah Morris. Of her we read that when she married Joseph

Richardson, her father, Anthony Morris, placed her in one scale, balancing her weight with gold in the other for a marriage dower. The family chronicle quaintly adds that the bride was of exceeding small stature.

Mrs. Earle, in her valuable and entertaining picture of New England customs and fashions, relates a somewhat similar incident in connection with the first marriage of Judge Sewall, except that in the latter case the bride was counted only worth her weight in silver. Her father, Captain Joseph Hull, gave the future Mrs. Sewall her dower in shillings, of the famous "pine-tree" brand.

Progressiveness among women, especially in business matters, is usually considered a nineteenth century departure, yet back in the days of the settlement of Pennsylvania we find Madame Mary Ferree taking up a tract of two thousand five hundred acres in what is now Lancaster County. Madame Ferree was the widow of John Ferree, a French gentleman of distinction. She fled to Germany to escape religious persecution in France, and, after spending two years in England, came to New York, and afterwards to Pennsylvania. While in England, Madame Ferree was presented to Queen Anne by William Penn, to whom she brought letters of introduction. From such luxuries and attractions as the Old World presented to one fitted to enjoy them, this heroic woman set forth with her family to make a home in what was then counted the wild west.

Another enterprising settler was Mrs. Duncan, from Scotland, whose name appears in early Philadelphia directories as "Margaret Duncan, Merchant, No. 1 S. Water Street." On her voyage to America the vessel in which Mrs. Duncan sailed was wrecked, and the passengers who took to the boats soon found that they had carried so little food with them that they were forced to draw lots in order to divide the scant supply. In an hour of great extremity, when there seemed small hope of rescue, Mrs. Duncan made a vow to build a church in her new home in the event of her deliverance. The "Vow Church" stood

on the west side of Thirteenth Street, north
of Market, and, like the Roman Catholics'

> " Votive frigate, soft aloft
> Riding in air this hundred years,
> Safe smiling at old hopes and fears,"

long bore witness to the faith, prosperity,
and gratitude of this good Presbyterian
settler of old Philadelphia.

A merchant princess from whom many
New Yorkers are descended was Margaret
Hardenbrook, who married, in 1659, Ru-
dolphus De Vries, an extensive trader of
New Amsterdam, and after his death became the wife of Frederick Philipse. During her widowhood Mrs. De Vries under-
took the management of her husband's
estate, which is said to have been a prac-
tice not uncommon in New Amsterdam,
and was early known as a woman trader,
going to Holland repeatedly in her own
ship as supercargo, and buying and trading
in her own name. After her second marriage, Mrs. Philipse still continued to man-
age her estate, and through his wife's thrift
and enterprise, as much as through his
own industry, Mr. Philipse soon came to

7*

be the richest man in the Colony, being
an extensive trader with the Five Nations
at Albany, and sending ships to both the
East and the West Indies.   From this
marriage of Margaret De Vries was descended Mary Philipse, whose chief claim
to distinction now rests upon the tradition
that she was an early love of Colonel
Washington's.

If in the days of the settlement there
were to be seen in Massachusetts and Pennsylvania interesting and notable women,
through all the Colonies we find their faces
and voices lending softer shadings to the
rugged scenes of pioneer life.   Many of
these women were the wives and daughters of Colonial governors, secretaries, and
chief justices, patroons and landed proprie-
tors.   Being of good birth and breeding,
and equipped with whatever intellectual
training was deemed suitable for a woman
in those days, they not only brought comfort and the sunshine of happiness into the
early homes of America, but also a certain
refinement and elevation of thought which
are most frequently a woman's donation

to the life around her. When we look into the faces of some of these Colonial Dames, as they have come down to us in portraits of the time, and read there the strength, nobility, and self-restraint that the lines disclose, we realize how much these women contributed towards the character-building that rendered the Revolutionary period an almost phenomenal epoch in the history of nations.

An interesting and significant circumstance in the settlement of Virginia is to be found in the fact that no women came over among the earliest colonists, as did those who came to make homes upon the more northern shores. " The Virginia pioneers were treated," says Mr. Drake, " not as men, but more as soldiers sent out to occupy an enemy's country." Does not this circumstance, taken in connection with the fact that " the painstaking men of arts and practices" needed for the settlement of a colony were wanting in this one, account for the failure of some of the early attempts at colonization in Virginia ? From the humbler walks of life there was sent

over to this colony, by Sir Edwin Sandys,
a number of young women of good character to be sold to such of the planters
as would take them for wives in payment of their passage money, the sum to
be paid in tobacco. Sir Edwin realized
that unless the settlements came to be
looked upon as a home they would not
succeed, notwithstanding all Virginia's
natural advantages, of which Raphe
Hamor wrote, " I know no one country
yielding, without art or industry, so many
fruits ; sure I am England does not." It
was considered a great event when a gentlewoman, Mistress Forrest, and her maid
came over with Newport in one of his
later voyages, especially as the maid,
Anne Burras, married one of the settlers,
John Laydon. In the manuscript records
of Maryland there are mentioned a Margaret and a Mary Brent, friends or relatives of Governor Leonard Calvert, who
visited the Isle of Kent accompanied by
Anne, a lame maid-servant of Sir Edward
Plowden. The fact that such arrivals as
these were chronicled as matters of im-

portance would seem to indicate that few gentlewomen came early to the Southern Colonies. Yet from the records of arrivals it appears that a number of women of the better class came to Virginia with their husbands between 1617 and 1624, while the Hamiltons and Chews, later residents of Pennsylvania, were early settlers in Maryland and Virginia. Later, there arose upon the banks of the James, the Potomac, and the Chesapeake, stately mansions surrounded by plantations that rivalled the parks of old England,—Shirley, Brandon, Westover, Gunston Hall, the home of the Masons, Flower de Hundred, Wyanoke, the Hermitage, Wye House,—names synonymous with generous living, hospitality, and all the charms with which refined womanhood adorns a home. It was to Ampthill, his country seat on the James River, that Archibald Cary brought his beautiful wife, Mary Randolph, an aunt of the famous John Randolph of Roanoke, and grandmother of Thomas Mann Randolph, Jr., Governor of Virginia.

An early Maryland settler was Madam

f

Anna Neale, whose husband was a man greatly trusted by Charles I. of England, while she was in the service of Queen Henrietta Maria as maid of honor. Among family heirlooms, still to be seen, are a large ring containing a miniature likeness of Charles I., and a pendant from a necklace, oval in form, set in brilliants and pearls, and encircling a figure of the Blessed Virgin standing under a crown upon a crescent, supported by the head of a cherub, all of which is supposed to be a representation of the Assumption. Both of these heirlooms were presents from the ill-fated royal couple of England. Nothing definite is known of Mrs. Neale's birth or parentage, although a family chronicle quaintly records that " it was not to her discredit that she was an American by birth, and a daughter of Benjamin Gynne (or Gill), a planter of Charles County, Maryland, where Captain Neale became acquainted with her and married her."*

* Later investigations incline us to the belief that Anna Gill was born in England, and probably married Captain Neale abroad, as she and her four children

Be this as it may, Captain and Mrs. Neale were both in England during the reign of Charles I., and much trusted by the royal family, the captain being sent by the king and the Duke of York on a secret mission to Spain. "The relations of a political nature," says the family narrative, "shown by this agency were such as to bring him into personal friendship with the king, and Mrs. Neale, through her husband's influence, into the service of the queen, and also warranted their asking and having the presence of her Majesty (by proxy) at the baptism of their eldest daughter, whom they were permitted to name 'Henrietta Maria,' in honor of her royal sponsor." *

After the execution of the king in 1648, Captain Neale brought his family to

---

were naturalized on coming to Maryland in 1666. One account of this lady tells us that she was a maid of honor at the court of Anne of Austria, which may have been true, as Queen Henrietta Maria took refuge with her royal sister-in-law in France, whither her maid of honor, Anna Gill, may have accompanied her.

* The Chamberlaine Family, by John Bezman Kerr.

Maryland, and purchased a tract of land in Charles County with Spanish coins known as "cob dollars," thus originating the name of Cob Neck, where he settled. From the union of these two romantic figures in the early history of Maryland have descended Lloyds, Tilghmans, Hollydays, Haywards, Goldsboroughs, Chamberlaines, Carrolls, Blakes, and Milnors, while fair Henrietta Marias in different generations have perpetuated the name of their royal godmother. From Captain James and Anna Neale came the distinguished Archbishop Neale, who was educated in France, ministered to Philadelphia and Baltimore parishes, and was later President of Georgetown College. Another noted descendant of Madam Neale was Charles Carroll, the barrister, who acted so important a part in early Revolutionary conventions in Maryland. His father, Dr. Charles Carroll, was of the great Irish house of Ely O'Carroll, while his mother was lovely Dorothy Blake, a grand-daughter of Anna Neale.

If few women came to Virginia in the first immigration, there were in 1676 wives and daughters who took sides with their husbands and fathers in the Great Rebellion, and, like the young wife of Major Cheeseman, had courage to face the cruel and despotic Berkeley. A few years earlier the first William Byrd had brought his English wife, Mary Horsmanden, to Westover, where his son William was born. Early in the next century Lady Spotswood accompanied her husband to what must have then seemed the outermost bounds of civilization, Germanna, Governor Spotswood's settlement of Germans upon the Rapidan, where he built the first iron furnace in North America.

"An enchanted castle," Colonel Byrd calls Germanna, of which he writes in his entertaining "Progress to the Mines,"—

" I arrived about three o'clock, and found only Mrs. Spotswood at home, who received her old acquaintance with many a gracious smile. I was carried into a room elegantly set off with pier glasses, the largest of which came soon after to an odd misfortune. Amongst other favourite animals that cheered this lady's solitude, a brace of tame deer ran familiarly about the house, and one of them came to stare at me as a stranger. But unluckily spying his own figure in the glass, he made a

8

spring over the tea-table that stood under it, and shat-
tered the glass to pieces, and, falling back upon the
tea-table, made a terrible fracas among the china. This
exploit was so sudden, and accompanied with such a
noise, that it surprised me, and perfectly frightened Mrs.
Spotswood.   But it was worth all the damage, to show
the moderation and good humour with which she bore
the disaster.   In the evening the noble colonel came
home from his mines, who saluted me very civilly, and
Mrs. Spotswood's sister, Miss Theky, who had been to
meet him *en cavalier*, was so kind too as to bid me
welcome. We talked over a legend of old stories,
supped about nine, and then prattled with the ladies till
it was time for a traveller to retire."

A pleasant picture Colonel Byrd has left
us of this good soldier and statesman,
whom he calls the Tubal Cain of Virginia,
discussing a bowl of " rack punch" and his
iron-making with the master of Westover,
or perchance unfolding to him his scheme
for reducing the mail communication between Williamsburg and Philadelphia to
eight days !* Colonel Byrd is disposed to
rally the doughty warrior upon his great

---

* Alexander Spotswood was Deputy Postmaster General for the Colonies from 1730 to 1739, and it was
through his influence that Benjamin Franklin was appointed Postmaster for Pennsylvania.

domesticity and devotion to Lady Spotswood, " rubbing up his memory" upon the
opposite maxims which he was wont to
preach before he was married, to which the
Governor replies, like the gallant gentleman that he is, " that whoever brings a
poor gentlewoman into so solitary a place
from all her friends and acquaintances,
would be ungrateful not to use her with all
possible tenderness."

Although Colonel Byrd is occasionally
inclined to sharpen his wits at the expense
of the fair sex, remarking of the conversation of the ladies at Germanna that it was
" like whip syllabub, very pretty, but had
nothing in it," while he discouragingly
alludes to Mrs. Chiswell as one of those
" absolute rarities, a very good old woman,"
and makes jokes that seem unsuited to so
courteous a gentleman upon Miss Theky
and her maiden state, which he describes
her as bewailing daily in a beautiful bower
upon Governor Spotswood's plantation,
he is quite ready to enjoy a Michaelmas
goose of the spinster's raising, and to find
much satisfaction in " the good company

of Mrs. Byrd and her little governor, my
son."

Those were days of unsavory witticisms,
and Colonel Byrd was only following the
example of some of the elegant gentlemen
with whom he had associated while com-
pleting his education in England. Mr. John
Dunton, who visited Boston a little earlier,
was capable of making remarks upon the
women whom he met that were worthy a
countryman of the caustic Pepys, although
his pen-pictures are usually flattering. Mrs.
Stewart's face, at thirty-three, he finds " a
magazine of beauty from whence she may
fetch artillery enough to wound a Thousand
Lovers," which makes his disapprobation
of Mrs. D., Doll S——, and others stand
out in stronger colors. The latter he calls
"a perpetual contradiction, made up of I
will and I will not;" while of another dame,
whose name he prudently omits, he ob-
serves that " she takes as much state upon
her, as wou'd have serv'd six of Queen
Elizabeth's Countesses; and yet she's no
Lady neither. . . . She seldom appears
twice in a shape; but every time she goes

abroad, puts on a different Garb. Had she been with the Israelites in the Wilderness, when for forty years their Cloaths wax'd not old, it had been punishment enough for her, to have gone so long in one fashion."

Fashion had certainly made great strides since the days of the early settlement if a woman could thus often change her "garb and shape." Judge Sewall might well bewail the advance into favor of the despised periwig, and if he one day experiences a melancholy pleasure in recording the fact that a periwig-maker and barber has died the death of a drunkard, he is pained soon after to hear Mr. Mather, in his pulpit, inveigh against those who "strain at a Gnat and swallow a Camel," who are "zealous against an innocent fashion, taken up and used by the best of men; and yet make no conscience of being guilty of great Immoralities." "'Tis supposed means wearing a Perriwig," says Sewall. "I expected not to hear a vindication of Perriwigs in Boston pulpit by Mr. Mather." Nor perhaps did Mr. Sewall expect to see in his

8*

own town of Salem a glaring advertise-
ment of elaborate wigs and coiffures for
both sexes. Even in Quaker Pennsylvania
such innovations began to obtain in the
next century, as we find Lewis Fay and
Louis Duchatêau informing the public,
through the journals of the day, that they
were qualified to " dress Ladies in fifty
different manners with their own natural
hair," while those ladies who had not
sufficient hair of their own, or were subject to headache, were consoled with the
promise that they could be " dressed with
false curls so well as not to be distinguished from their natural ones." These
accomplished artists also assured their pa-
trons that they " set on brilliants or flowers to the greatest advantage," and, not to
neglect the adornment of the sterner sex,
engaged " to dress Gentlemen's hair in
thirty fashionable and different manners
agreeable to their faces and airs."

This sounds like gayety and frivolity ; yet
although the dignified men in satin coats
and lace ruffles who look down upon this
generation from the canvases of Black-

burn, Smibert, his pupil John Copley,* and from those of Stuart, West, Peale, and Trumbull, were very elegant gentlemen, they were also industrious, God-fearing men and law-abiding citizens. The ladies, their pendants upon the wall, if they were *grandes dames* in a certain sense, and upon gala days appeared stiff and elegant in their brocades and satins, with hair towering high or tortured into innumerable curls and rings, were far from frivolous as a rule,

---

* In none of his paintings does Copley more fully display the grace and breadth of treatment which were the distinguishing characteristics of his best work than in the group of his own family. In this picture Mrs. Copley leans forward to caress her boy, whose hand is laid confidingly upon his mother's cheek, while the little maid in the foreground presents a charming combination of childish innocence and dignity. This painting possesses a more than ordinary historic interest, as the older gentleman standing near Mr. Copley, his father-in-law, is the Mr. Richard Clarke who refused to return the tea consigned to him in 1774, and may thus, in a certain sense, be considered the originator of the Boston tea party, the boy whom Mrs. Copley bends over is the future Lord Chancellor of England, and the little girl, Elizabeth, is looked upon with interest by many Bostonians as their ancestress, Mrs. Gardiner Greene.

and if an occasional ball or play diversified
the monotony of their days, the majority of
them were spent as Mr. Swanwick describes
the excellent Maria spending hers :

> "No gadding frenzy takes her choice,
> But strictly ruled by reason's voice
> She finds no bliss to roam.
> *   *   *   *   *
> No hideous dress this fair one wears,
> Not fashions but a mother's cares
> Engross her every hour."

Indeed, domesticity was a necessity as
well as a virtue in Colonial and Provincial
life, and while, as Mr. Dunton remarked
of Mrs. William Stewart, of Boston, " Her
pride was to be Neat and Cleanly, and her
thrift not to be Prodigal, which made her
seldom a non-resident of her household,"
the Southern matron gathered her slaves
about her and instructed them in cooking,
sewing, and all domestic arts. The woman
of the olden time was skilled in the use of
her needle, in embroidery, lace-making, and
all manner of fine needle-work. Little
Miss Swift wrote from Boston to her papa
and mamma in Philadelphia of spending

hours at her " Tam Bar frame," while a
pretty picture has come down to us of the
young girls sitting out upon Boston Common in the afternoon with their spinning-
wheels before them, industry being the
fashion in Colonial days. A not unat-
tractive scene this to the traveller, who
was taken to witness the latest Boston
device for combining the useful and the
beautiful! " The Government being in the
hands of Dissenters they don't admit of
Plays, or Musick - houses," wrote Mr.
Bennet, but here is a series of attractive
tableaux vivants en plein air, bevies of girls
laying their hands to the spindle, like
King Solomon's model housewife, or as
Mr. Longfellow pictured the captivating
maiden of Plymouth :

" Seated beside her wheel, and the carded wool like a
    snow-drift
  Piled at her knee, her white hands feeding the raven-
    ous spindle,
  While, her foot on the treadle, she guided the wheel
    in its motion."

These girls doubtless covered themselves with what good Mr. Whitefield called

" The Pride of Life," and indulged in as much innocent rivalry over caps and gowns as over the number of hanks of flax and wool spun, for young people seemed to be young even in New England, and quite as tender glances of sweethearts could be exchanged over spinning-wheels as in the pauses of the dance in gayer circles.

A descendant of Thomas Jefferson's Belinda writes of the Virginia lady of the olden time, " Very little from books was thought necessary for a girl. She was trained to domestic matters, however, must learn the accomplishments of the day, to play upon the harpsichord or spinet, and to work impossible dragons and roses on canvas." Bits of embroidery still preserved testify to the skill of olden-time ladies. Mrs. Washington was a notable needlewoman, and paintings on velvet and satin, and pictures executed in silk and chenille by her grand - daughter, Nellie Custis, prove that she was an adept in such girlish accomplishments. Nor was the busy needle applied to ornamental work alone ; it was far more useful than the pen, and almost as powerful as the sword, in those days of early home-making. Mr. Thomas Nelson Page, in his charming retrospective study of Virginia life, tells us how, when her husband complained of the gate being broken, the industrious mistress of the household promptly replied, "Well, my dear, if I could sew it with my needle and thread, I would mend it for you."

The olden-time girl, except in the home of the Puritan and the Quaker, was taught to dance as well as to use her needle, and in the Southern Colonies the former accomplishment was considered so important a part of the education of a young lady that Mr. Jefferson insisted that his daughter Martha should dance three days in the week, from eleven until one. Dr. Franklin also expressed great interest in Sally's dancing and playing upon the harpsichord, although he stipulated that she should improve her mind by reading "The Whole Duty of Man" and "The Young Lady's Library." That less instructive literature than this sometimes fell into the hands of the Colonial maiden, we learn from the diaries of Lucinda of Virginia and Sarah Eve. The former takes herself to task for being so fond of novel-reading, while Miss Eve pronounces "The Fashionable Lover" a prodigious fine comedy.

In addition to her lighter accomplishments the Colonial lady was an excellent housekeeper, in days when housekeeping meant having everything prepared under the supervision of the mistress of the home, from the cutting up of the pork and beef until the culminating moment when the sausages and mince pies appeared upon the table. There were in many of the old houses retinues of servants, and in the Middle and Southern Colonies slaves to do the bidding of the mistress, but everything had to be superintended by her; consequently in some of the old letters that come to us we find numerous homely domestic details, and great rejoicing over any small luxury or labor-saving device that found its way into the hands of the busy *châtelaine*. When travellers wrote of sumptuous dinners in hospitable South-

ern homes, or when Mr. William Black
told how he was feasted in Annapolis, or
when Silas Deane described an elaborate
dinner at the house of Miers Fisher in
Philadelphia, they little knew what the
preparation and arrangement of such a
menu meant to the mistress of the household, in days when she could not send
around the corner for the latest device
in confectionery with which to grace her
board, and when the syllabubs and cus-
tards were often prepared by the same
dainty hands that served them to her
guests.

A pleasant story is told of Mrs. Clement
Biddle, a worthy descendant of pioneer
women of Rhode Island. Mrs. Biddle was
with her husband in the Valley Forge encampment, and when an order was issued
that the officers' wives should leave the
camp, she, with ready tact and skill, prepared so delectable a dinner for General
Washington and his staff that the order
was not carried out in her case, showing
that the heroes of the Revolution were not
insensible to the seductions of such good

E   *g.*   9

cheer as a notable Philadelphia housewife
knew how to set before the masculine de-
vourer. The story runs that as Mrs. Biddle
rose from the table, she airily remarked
that she had heard of the order, but felt
sure that the General would not apply it to
her, to which charmingly feminine speech
the Commander-in-Chief, bowing low, replied, " Certainly not to Mrs. Biddle."

Bradstreet House, North Andover, Mass.

A GROUP OF EARLY POETESSES.

AMONG the early settlers of the Colonies there was, occasionally, a woman of more than ordinary intelligence, and now and again a ready writer or a verse-maker. Perhaps in all the settlements, North and South, there was no woman equal in mind and spirit to Anne Hutchinson, whom even her enemies acknowledged to be " a masterpiece of woman's wit."

Enthusiasm, unrestrained by tact or worldly considerations, a strain of headstrongness in her religious fervor, and a power of carrying with her the minds and hearts of her hearers, were apparently the leading characteristics of this devoted young woman, the latter trait being perhaps the most difficult for her persecutors to overlook. From the grim travesty of

that trial in which Winthrop, Dudley, Endicott, and other worthies, who had come to
the New World for freedom of thought and
action, sat in judgment upon one against
whom the only charge made was that she
exercised this coveted freedom in her life
and teaching, we turn with a mingled sense
of shame and regret,—shame that men who
had come hither for such high purposes
could stoop to deeds so unworthy, and
regret that a creature of such noble
spirit should have been so misunderstood.
Had Anne Hutchinson found her way to
America half a century later, with the followers of Penn, we can readily imagine the
career of usefulness and honor that would
have opened for her.

The more tolerant doctrine of the inner
light found no place in the spiritual furniture of those who had shaken off the iron
hand of a State Church, and when we
look back upon the dealings of the early
Puritans with one another it seems as if
the rule that "might makes right" was as
stoutly maintained in New England as in
the feudal life of older England.

In the same community that condemned and banished Anne Hutchinson for her teaching of " dangerous doctrine,"* we find another attractive womanly personality, Anne Bradstreet, who is spoken of in the first London edition of her poems as " The Tenth Muse Lately Sprung up in America," † but who is dearer to us as our first poetess, singing like a lark in the chill New England morn. Her verses we may not care to read now; although they are characterized by considerable poetic thought and by some graces of poetic treatment, besides bearing marks of an early acquaintance with the great English writers of the past century, some of whom were still living while little Anne Dudley was " lisping

---

* " Mrs. Hutchinson's custom seems to have been to report the discourses of Mr. John Cotton, and to impress their lessons upon her hearers. In the progress of the discussion the sermons of other ministers were commented upon, and finally her own views presented."— *Memorial History of Boston*, iv. 334.

† The poetess is also spoken of by an English admirer as " Mistress *Anne Bradstreet, at present residing in the Occidental parts of the world* in America, alias NOV-ANGLIA."

9*

in numbers," if dealing in numbers at all.
To uncongenial surroundings and houses
ill fitted to protect the settlers from the
bleak winds and storms of a New England
winter came Mrs. Bradstreet, from an English home of the better class, which, if
boasting few of the luxuries of to-day, was
sufficiently comfortable in its appointments
to form a strong contrast to the dwellings
of the early settlers of Massachusetts.
Sensitive, delicately nurtured, her mind
always in advance of her frail body, her
first American experiences being the illness and death of her friend and fellow-
voyager, the lovely Lady Arbella Johnson,
and the drowning of young Henry Winthrop, it is not strange that one of Mrs.
Bradstreet's earliest poems should have
been upon " A Fit of Sickness," nor that
it should have been followed a few months
later by a joyous outburst of song upon
the approach of spring:

> " As spring the winter doth succeed,
>   And leaves the naked trees doe dresse,
>   The earth all black is cloth'd in green ;
>   At sunshine each their joy expresse.

" My winters past, my stormes are gone,
　　And former cloudes seem now all fled ;
But, if they must eclipse again,
　　I'll run where I was succored."

What this first spring must have been to
these pilgrims when they beheld the gray
hill-sides and snow-bound valleys covered
with verdure and bloom, and " replenished
with thick woods and high trees," we learn
from the expressions of that quaint and
amusing chronicler, Francis Higginson.

Disposed to make the best of everything, this worthy divine rejoiced alike over
the trials and hardships that were good for
his soul, and the dainty springs, luscious
lobsters, and sweet and wholesome bass
that sustained his mortal body, finding here
an " increase of corne, which proved this
country to be a wonderment, which outstript
Joseph's increase in Egypt." Yet, great as
was this increase, it was not sufficient to
outlast the long stagnation of the winter,
when the cold was so great that Judge
Sewall tells of the sacramental bread being
frozen upon the plate, and when Judge
Lynde was in the habit of driving across

Penny's ferry on the ice. A realization of what was suffered by the youngest members of the community is emphasized by the sight of a pair of christening mittens worn in his babyhood by an early governor of Massachusetts, which were certainly needed in churches where fire was unknown,—except perhaps as a figure of speech in the pulpit.

"The bright and at times almost tropical summers of New England must have been the salvation of the colonists," says Mr. Lodge. "Nothing else broke the gloom. There were absolutely no amusements of any kind, and although establishing great political and religious principles and founding States are the noblest tasks to which men can set their hands, yet poor humanity requires some relaxation. Nature's winter was severe, but it lasted only for a season, while the social winter was never broken until the whole system began to give way in the next century."

From this chilling atmosphere, Anne Bradstreet wrote, at the age of nineteen,—

" Twice ten years old not fully told since nature gave me
      breath,
My race is run, my thread is spun, lo ! here is fatal
      Death."

That her race was not run, and that Mrs. Bradstreet lived to be more than three times nineteen, and the happy mother of eight children, does not detract from the pathos of these youthful lines.

Whatever gifts may have been Anne Bradstreet's possession, we may believe that they had small space for expansion in a community that fed with avidity upon such mental pabulum as " The Simple Cobbler of Agawam," and later upon Wigglesworth's " Day of Doom," with its descriptions, worthy the advanced realist of to-day. In the latter work the author descants upon the sufferings of the condemned and of the unelect infants, who, although assured that their sins were not equal to those of the hardened reprobate, were told, poor babes, that for the crime of coming into this world at all, there apparently being no other,—

" Therefore in bliss
You may not hope to dwell ;
But unto you I shall allow
The easiest room in hell."

That Mrs. Bradstreet should have risen
above the depressing influence of her life
and surroundings enough to sing at all is
sufficient wonder, not that her notes should
have been tinged with the melancholy of
the prevailing atmosphere.   It is to be re-
gretted that she did not more frequently
turn from the introspective studies that
engaged her pen, and from such time-worn
themes as the Four Seasons, the Four Elements, and Ancient Monarchies, to describe events and impressions belonging to
the new life around her.   This was a time
when some picturesque personalities were
abroad, and if the persecutions of Quakers
and other independent thinkers have presented scenes sufficiently stirring to arouse
the fancy of later poets and dramatists, it
seems strange that they failed to inspire
this most sensitive and imaginative woman.

It should perhaps be remembered that
those were days when women were less

accustomed to giving their opinions upon
public matters than now, while another
and a stronger reason for Mrs. Bradstreet's silence upon these burning ques-
tions is to be found in the fact that Governor Dudley and Simon Bradstreet were
both engaged in the trials of Anne Hutchinson and of the Quakers, the latter, be it
said to his credit, with far less malignity
than the former.* Although Anne Bradstreet's loyalty to her father and husband
seems to have kept her pen silent when
her spirit must often have rebelled, she
had enough vigor left in her frail body
to utter her protest against the carping
tongues that thought a needle fitted her
hand better than a pen, vindicating her
woman's right to be a poet by quoting the
Greeks, whose muses nine were embodied
in woman's form,

" And poesy made *Calliope's* own child."

When Mrs. Bradstreet touches upon nature
and life, as she occasionally does in " Con-

---

* For some incidents in Mrs. Bradstreet's life we
are indebted to Helen Campbell's charming study of
" Anne Bradstreet and Her Times."

templations," and in her few domestic
poems, she reveals a much finer literary
quality, besides giving the reader a glimpse
of her tender nature and passionate woman's
heart. During one of Governor Bradstreet's
enforced absences from their Ipswich home
his wife wrote,—

" My head, my heart, mine Eyes, my life, my more,
    My joy, my Magazine of earthly store.
    If two be one as surely thou and I,
    How stayest thou there, whilst I at Ipswich lye ?"

Again she says,—

" As Loving Hind (Hartless) wants her Deer,
    Scuds through the woods and Fern with hearkening
        ear,
    Perplext in every bush and nook doth pry,
    Her dearest Deer might answer ear or eye."

It is pleasant to know that if Mrs. Bradstreet likened herself to his " Hind," his
" Mullet," and his " Dove," Simon Bradstreet was in some measure worthy of his
wife's devotion, being far more liberal-
minded and kindly by nature than were
most of those who surrounded him, and a
personable man withal, if one may judge
from his portrait. His affection for his

wife was so strong that after her death in 1675 he remained a widower for three years, a long period of mourning for a wife in Puritan New England.

One of Mrs. Bradstreet's poems, in which she describes her children as " eight birds hatcht in one nest," is suggestive of Chaucer in its quaint simplicity and in the writer's skilful handling of homely details. This poem was written some years after the Bradstreets removed to Andover, and is, as Mrs. Campbell says, a sort of family biography. Some of the older children were married and settled in their own homes, while the younger ones still " nested" with their mother. In view of her eldest son's leaving home, Mrs. Bradstreet beseeches him to

> " Fly back and sing amidst this Quire,"

while the little ones, still in the nest, she thus admonishes with tender bird-mother solicitude :

> " Alas, my birds, you wisdome want,
>   Of perils you are ignorant ;
>   Oft times in grass, on trees, in flight,
>   Sore accidents on you may light."

10

Through the entire poem, which is quite long, the writer never drops or mixes her figures, even when she recounts the dangers to which her brood is likely to be exposed, as in the lines,—

"If birds could weep, then would my tears
    Let others know what are my fears
    Lest this my brood some harm should catch,
    And be surpriz'd for want of watch,
    Whilst pecking corn, and void of care
    They fall un'wares in Fowler's snare;
    Or whilst on trees they sit and sing,
    Some untoward boy at them do fling;
    Or whilst allur'd with bell and glass,
    The net be spread, and caught, alas.
    Or least by Lime-twigs they be foyl'd,
    Or by some greedy hawks be spoyl'd.
    O, would my young, ye saw my breast,
    And knew what thoughts there sadly rest.
    Great was my pain when I you bred,
    Great was my care when I you fed,
    Long did I keep you soft and warm,
    And with my wings kept off all harm."

If this mother, whose heart was filled with such trembling solicitude for the future of her brood, could have realized that from the home-nest at Andover were to descend such lights in literature and theology as the Channings, the Danas, Wendell Phillips, and Dr. Oliver Wendell Holmes, the strain with which she closed her poem might have been more exultant, but could have been no more earnest:

> "Thus gone, amongst you I may live,
> And dead, yet speak, and counsel give;
> Farewel, my birds farewel, adieu,
> I happy am, if well with you."

Another New England poetess, of a much later date, was Mercy Warren, daughter of James Otis, of Barnstable, and wife of James Warren, sometime President of the Provincial Congress of Massachusetts.* This lady, whom her friend Mrs. Winthrop addressed as Philomela, wrote a number of poems and tragedies abounding in the classical allusions

---

* George Sandys was writing verses and translating Ovid on the banks of the James ten years before Anne Bradstreet came to Massachusetts. Yet in the years that followed, the muse of poetry was more prone to frequent the New England Colonies than those of Virginia and Maryland, although no more inspiring themes could be found than histories as romantic as that of Evelyn Byrd, and faces as beautiful as those of Mary Randolph, Anne Francis, and Dorothy Blake.

so common at that time.   Political reveries
in verse also engaged her pen, and spirited
attacks upon the manners and customs of
the day, in which

> " India's poisonous weed,
>   Long since a sacrifice to Thetis made,"

came in for a full share of her keen satire.
Mrs. Warren also left a number of admirable pen-pictures of the great men of the
day, clear, sharp, and well drawn.   It is
interesting to learn from one of her letters,
written during the encampment at Cambridge, that she considered General Washington "the most amiable and accomplished gentleman both in person, mind
and manners that she has ever met with,"
and equally so to know that her first impression of Charles Lee was far less favorable, and that she found him, with all his
learning and ability, "plain in his person
to a degree of ugliness and careless even
to unpoliteness."

Nor were the visits of the muse con-
fined to the Colonial and Provincial women
of New England, as we learn that down

in Pennsylvania Elizabeth Fergusson was composing poetry about the same time as Mrs. Warren, while Mrs. Deborah Logan, a little later, was writing both prose and verse, the former destined to survive the latter, not only because it was more excellent, but also because it gives us pictures of the times, a form of composition whose value, like wine, increases with the years. Susanna Wright, Hannah Griffitts, a grand-daughter of the first Isaac Norris, and Mrs. Richard Stockton were among our early poetesses. The latter, born Annis Boudinot, a New Jersey woman, composed verses upon "Peace," upon "The Surrender of Cornwallis," and a triumphal ode to the Commander-in-Chief. The letters in which Washington thanked Mrs. Stockton for these patriotic poems are among the most charming and playful to be found in his correspondence, and, if somewhat more ponderous than similar effusions in our day, are interesting as illustrations of what the great man could do upon occasions when fancy held the rein. The poetess modestly sent a

line of apology with her verses, to which
the hero who inspired her muse thus
replied :

"You apply to me, my dear madam, for absolution,
as though I was your father confessor, and as though
you had committed a crime great in itself, yet of the
venial class.   You have reason good; for I find myself
strangely disposed to be a very indulgent ghostly adviser
upon this occasion, and notwithstanding 'you are the
most offending soul alive' (that is, if it is a crime to write
elegant poetry), yet if you will come and dine with me
on Thursday, and go through the proper course of peni-
tence which shall be prescribed, I will strive hard to
assist you in expiating these poetical trespasses on this
side of purgatory."

Mr. and Mrs. Stockton were evidently
a most congenial and devoted couple.   In
their letters they frequently addressed each
other as " Lucius" and " Emilia," after
the fanciful custom of the day.   Some of
these letters, written while Mr. Stockton
was in London in 1766, engaged with Dr.
Franklin in furthering the interests of the
Colonies, give us pleasing glimpses of the
wife, as seen through glasses that were
prone to magnify rather than to diminish
her charms.   Mrs. Stockton had declined
to accompany her husband abroad, because

she was unwilling to leave her children, or, as she expressed it, she felt "no particular call of Providence to venture both their parents in one bottom," and in all Mr. Stockton's letters, whether describing the royalties or such notable political figures as Chatham and Grenville, or in preparing for his wife a plan of Mr. Pope's gardens and grotto at Twickenham, there runs a thread of regret that one so fitted by taste and cultivation to appreciate Old World sights and sounds should not be enjoying them with him. After descanting upon the glories of the queen's birthnight ball, which was opened by some of the royalties and graced by the presence of the Duchesses of Bolton, Ancaster, Hamilton, and all the other famous beauties, he concludes, "But here I have done with the subject, for I had rather wander with you along the rivulets of Morven or Red Hill, and see the rural sports of the chaste little frogs, than again be at a birthnight ball." In another letter, Lucius speaks of his Emilia's poems, desiring her to send him some of the pieces he most admired, adding,

"I shall like much to have them to spell over for my amusement on my passage home." Although Mrs. Stockton was very modest about her effusions, and shrank from the notoriety of print, Mrs. Fergusson speaks of her, in one of her own poems, as the writer of many pleasing verses:

> "Here flow the good Emilia's strains
> In Morven's rural bowers."

One of Mrs. Stockton's daughters, Julia, married the distinguished Dr. Benjamin Rush, and another, Mary, became the wife of Andrew Hunter, of Virginia, who was publicly thanked by General Washington for his gallant service in the battle of Monmouth.

Elizabeth Fergusson did not write patriotic verses, as she was allied by birth and marriage with the Tory side of the question, being the grand-daughter of Lady Anne Keith,* second wife of Sir William

---

* Mrs. Fergusson was not the grand-daughter of Sir William Keith, as has been so often stated, but of his wife. By her first husband, Robert Diggs, Lady Keith had a daughter Anne, who married Dr. Thomas Graeme, of Philadelphia.

Keith, Penn's last deputy governor, and the wife of Hugh Fergusson, British Commissioner of Prisoners.

The story of Mrs. Fergusson having, in the early days of the Revolution, been a medium of communication between Governor Johnson and the American authorities, with a view to the bringing about of peace negotiations, is well known, and yet her part in the affair has never been thoroughly understood. She says that she "looked upon Governor Johnson as a friend to America who wished some person to step forth and act a mediatorial part, and suggest something to stop the effusion of blood which was likely to ensue if the war was carried on in full vigor." We can understand that Mrs. Fergusson's humanity, aside from any Tory proclivities, would naturally lead her to desire to bring about such a consummation; but that a woman of her mind and character should have allowed herself, with her eyes open, to engage in a transaction in which ten thousand guineas and a good post in the British government were offered to an American general in reward

for his services, is difficult to explain. We
can do no better than accept Mrs. Fergusson's own interpretation of the matter,
and conclude that she was ignorant of the
grosser details of the transaction, and
thought only of the desired result. " I
own," she says in one place, " I find it
hard, knowing the uncorruptness of my
own heart, to be held out to the public
as a tool to the commissioners. But the
impression is now made, and it is too late
to recall it." Much of the unpleasantness
of the association of this affair with her
name, Mrs. Fergusson was able to dispel
later by her own narrative, prepared as
a refutation of Governor Johnson's state-
ments. The fact also that so patriotic a
contemporary as Dr. Rush spoke with
unqualified praise of the woman, as well
as of the writer, leads us to believe that
Mrs. Fergusson's motives were understood and respected by those who knew
her best.

From this rather involved page of personal history it is pleasant to turn to an
earlier phase of this woman's life, when, as

the young daughter of Dr. Thomas Graeme; she assisted her father and mother to dispense the charming hospitality that rendered Graeme Park * a favorite resort of the cultivated men and women of the day, or amid its lovely groves composed the verses that made her one of the foremost American poets of her time. Miss Graeme's tastes were distinctly literary. In addition to her original poems, she translated Telemachus into English verse, while of her prose writings Dr. Rush wrote that they indicated "strong marks of genius, taste, and knowledge. Nothing," he says, "that came from her pen was common;" to which a no less capable critic than Mr. Joshua Francis Fisher added his meed of praise.

Although Miss Graeme, under the pseudonyme of "Laura," sometimes indulged in elegiac strains, and, like most

---

* Graeme Park is in Montgomery County, about nineteen miles from Philadelphia; the land on which the house was built was originally owned by Samuel Carpenter. Dr. Thomas Graeme bought the estate from Sir William Keith.

young poets, sighed for sadness and solitude, choosing for her retreat

"Some moss-grown cave,
Where oozing creeping waters flow,"

a delicate humor marks many of her
verses, especially those that resulted
from her friendship with the Rev. Nathaniel Evans.   In 1764, Miss Graeme
sailed for Europe with the Rev. Richard
Peters, rector of Christ Church, Philadelphia, in whose care she had been placed
by her parents.   While in London the
young poetess met many persons of distinction, among others the celebrated Dr.
John Fothergill, who became her friend as
well as her physician.   Calling to see her
one March day in 1765, Dr. Fothergill
exclaimed, "Yesterday you were made a
slave of, Betsey," to which she, girl-like,
suspecting some raillery on the subject
of matrimony, replied, "No, sir, I am a
slave to no man; my heart is my own."
"No, no, heart has nothing to do with
it," said the doctor, explaining that he referred to the passage of the Stamp Act,

which made her and her countrymen slaves of Great Britain.

On her return voyage Miss Graeme met the Rev. Nathaniel Evans, between whom and herself there soon grew up a strong liking. Whether or not Miss Graeme's heart was involved in this friendship it is difficult to say. That Mr. Evans succumbed to the charms of the young poetess his verses plainly revealed; certainly his death, at the age of twenty-five, closed a chapter which left its impress upon her future career. Soon after his return from abroad, Mr. Evans, who was in delicate health, was advised by his kindly physician, Dr. Graeme, to spend a part of the spring at Graeme Park; hence the following verse:

> " Thus musing o'er the charming plains,
>   Where Graeme the good and just retires,
>   Where Laura breathes her tender strains,
>   Where every graceful muse inspires."

An attractive setting this for the pastoral of parson and poetess ! Even now Graeme Park has a charm of its own ; much more in Colonial days, when the fine old house,

F   11

built by Governor Keith for his own residence, and surrounded by three hundred
acres of wooded park, double-ditched and
hedged in approved English fashion, with
sheep and cattle grazing upon its verdant
slopes, was the pride of the neighborhood.
Although the friendship destined to end
so sadly began gayly enough with jesting
and good-humored raillery, there is a
deeper tone in the man's verses than in the
woman's ; and if the rhymed badinage of
this couple recalls to us, as it did to the
writers themselves, the friendship of Swift
and Stella, we must transpose our characters, as in the case of the American pair it
was the woman who carrried off the palm
by the keenness and brilliancy of her satire.
Swift cruelly reminded Stella that her
dancing days were over, and, in verses addressed to her upon her birthday, wondered
how an angel would look at thirty-six ; but
it was Miss Graeme, " Laura," who satirized
some of her reverend friend's foibles so
cleverly in her " Country Parson" that he
was quick to recognize his own portrait in
the dominie of whom she wrote :

" Of manners gentle, and of temper even,
    He jogs his flock, with easy pace, to heaven.
    In Greek and Latin, pious books he keeps ;
    And, while his clerk sings psalms, he—soundly sleeps.
    His garden fronts the sun's sweet orient beams,
    And fat church-wardens prompt his golden dreams.
    From rustic bridegroom oft he takes the ring ;
    And hears the milk-maid plaintive ballads sing.
    Back-gammon cheats whole winter nights away,
    And Pilgrim's Progress helps a rainy day."

These piquant lines, modelled after Mr.
Pope's " Happy Life of a Country Parson,"
were received by young Evans thus good-
humoredly :

    " I lately saw, no matter where,
        A parody by Laura fair ;
        In which, beyond dispute, 'tis clear
        She means her country friend to jeer.
        For, well she knows, her pleasing lays,
        (Whether they banter me or praise,
        Whatever merry mood they take,)
        Are welcome for their author's sake."

To this Laura promptly replied that the
parson had no reason to flatter himself that
he was the subject from which she had
made her sketch ; and thus, the gage being
thrown down, the merry war was waged
through a number of sparkling verses.

This graceful little idyl at Graeme Park affords a pleasing contrast to the public life of the time, when heated political discussions upon the respective rights and wrongs of king and colonies were beginning to stir men's minds, North and South. Against the dark background of war and suffering soon to follow, it stands out in the clear spring air like a bit of Arcadia transported to the New World. So it must have appeared in the retrospect to Elizabeth Graeme, to whose later years many troubles came, whose marriage to Hugh Fergusson, against her father's wishes, seems to have brought her little happiness, and who solaced her lonely heart by her studies and translations, instead of, like Anne Bradstreet, stringing together rhymes upon children who gathered around her knees.

Mantel of the Robinson House Newport R.I.

COLONIAL DAMES.

MRS. KNOWLES, the ingenious Quaker lady who outwitted Dr. Johnson in more than one tilt of words, illustrated her theories upon the education of women by citing the happy consequences of a woman's understanding the reason for the bursting of a pudding-bag, describing her as she "calms her maids by learned disquisitions and proceeds to make a fresh pudding out of the mixture; whereas the ignorant housewife thinks a hobgoblin is in the pot, and gets into a perfect state of flurry."

Placing the question upon a higher ground than pudding-making, we find a Pennsylvania pedagogue, in 1765, proposing to teach young ladies "true spelling with the rules for pointing with propriety," urging upon them not to be discouraged on account of their age, or through fear of obtaining a spouse, as he has had "the honour to give the finishing stroke in education to several of the reputed fine accomplished ladies in New York, some of which were married within two, three and four years afterwards." Truly the ambitious instructor proved his right to be patronized!

All through the days of the settlement, whether learned or unlearned, women had been proving the superiority of mind over matter by the ingenuity and fertility of resource with which they overcame difficulties and brought comfort out of chaos. From that early and solitary Virginia witch, Grace Sherwood, who outwitted her persecutors by swimming when she was expected to sink, to the high-born and patriotic dames of North Carolina who banded themselves together to drink a decoction of raspberry leaves instead of tea until the odious tax should be taken off,* Colonial women faced perils and difficulties with unfailing heroism and patience. "To find a way or make one" seemed to be the motto of the hour. Danger developed latent courage, and emergency seemed to whet mother-wit to keener edge, as when Lydia Darrach set out upon her lonely walk through a country filled with the enemy's troops, or when Mrs. Philip Schuyler, hearing that the British soldiers were on their

---

* This association, formed in October, 1774, was presided over by Mrs. Penelope Barker, and joined by Mrs. Elizabeth King, Mrs. Sarah Valentine, Miss Isabella Johnston, a sister of Governor Johnston, of North Carolina, Mrs. Hoskins, and forty-six other women, who signed a paper which read as follows: "We the Ladys of Edenton do hereby solemnly engage not to Conform to that Pernicious Custom of Drinking Tea, or that we the aforesaid Ladys will not promote ye wear of any manufacture from England, untill such time that all Acts which tend to enslave our Native Country shall be repealed."—"The Historic Tea Party of Edenton," by Richard Dillard.

way to Schuylerville to secure her absent husband's crop of grain, set fire to the fields with her own hands, rather than suffer such aid and comfort to fall to the share of the enemy; or as when Madam Hancock ordered all the stray cows on the Common to be milked because the Honorable John brought home to breakfast a larger company of officers than her larder could supply.   Equally clever and prompt to take advantage of the situation was the Widow Nice, who, when the British officers quartered upon her at the Rising Sun Tavern complained of the butter, remarked that she could probably get better if she had a horse to ride out into the country in search of it.   Being provided with a horse, the good lady took the precaution to secure some of her valuables in her saddle-bags, and, thus equipped, rode off upon her confiscated steed, to return no more until Philadelphia was in possession of the Continentals.

Well might Abigail Adams write from her Braintree home, where she lived in constant dread of hostilities and was often in want of the ordinary comforts of life, to her husband in Philadelphia, who was helping to "usher in the birth of a fine boy," as he playfully dubbed the Declaration of '76,—

"And by the way in the new code of laws, which I suppose it would be necessary to make, I desire you to remember the ladies, and be more generous and favorable to them than your ancestors were. Do not put such an unlimited power into the hands of the husbands. Remember all men would be tyrants if they could. If particular care and attention are not paid to the ladies, we are determined to foment a rebellion, and will not hold ourselves bound by any laws in which we have no voice or representation."

Although these remarks produced no effect upon the worthy framers of the Declaration, in which respect they remind us of a number of similar manifestoes that have followed them, they are interesting because of their independence of spirit, showing from what quarter the wind blew in Boston even in early days.

"If we mean to have heroes, statesmen, and philosophers, we should have learned women," writes Mrs. Adams upon another

occasion, which looks as if she had already
grasped the favorite theory of the modern
scientist, that great men are usually the
sons of superior mothers. History has
presented such meagre outlines of the
mothers of the Republic that we turn to
letters and diaries for the more intimate
touches that reveal character and give the
key-note to the situation; as when we
learn that Jane Randolph, the bride of
Peter Jefferson, rode behind her husband
to his pioneer home in the primeval forest,
she having been bred in whatever luxury
belonged to the Colonial life of Virginia;
or gather from family records some idea
of the mingled austerity and affection of
the home life of the young Washingtons.
More than history reveals we wish to
know of the mother who in girlhood was
the belle of the countryside, but who in
her early widowhood devoted all her time
and thought to the training of her children and the management of the estate
that had been left to them.

Although Mary Washington and Abiah
Franklin are chiefly known to later gen-

erations as the mothers of great sons, it
is evident that both of these women were
possessed of strong character and distinct
individuality. Firmness, moderation, and
deep religious sentiment were leading traits
of Mrs. Washington; while Mrs. Franklin,
thrifty and hard-working, having at two-
and-twenty undertaken Josiah Franklin
with his brood of little children, which
her own contribution of ten augmented
to the goodly number of sixteen, still
found time, like a true daughter of New
England, to reflect upon theological ques-
tions. Dr. Franklin says in one of his
letters that his mother "grieves that one
of her sons is an Arian and the other
an Arminian, although what these terms
mean I do not very well know." Mrs.
Franklin probably knew what she meant,
and was decided in her opinions, having
been reared in an atmosphere of theological discussion, her father, Peter Folger,
being a scholar and a man far in advance
of his time in religious thought. That
the mother was not rigid in her ideas of
life is evident from the freedom with which

her son tells her of his own sayings and doings and of his daughter Sally's learning to play the harpsichord and to dance. Writing to Dr. Franklin soon after his election to the Common Council of Philadelphia, Mrs. Franklin begs him " to look up to God and thank him for all his good Providences," expressing her satisfaction that he is " so well respected in his town that they chose" him " an Alderman," adding, with a shrewdness not unlike her son's, " Altho' I don't know what it means, or what the better you will be of it besides the honor."

A not unworthy daughter-in-law of the thrifty mistress of the Blue Ball was Deborah Reed, the wife of Benjamin Franklin, whose dignity, discretion, and great patience during the long absences abroad of her " dear child" entitle her to the respect and admiration of those who revere her more brilliantly endowed husband. That she inspired both of these sentiments in the mind of the great philosopher is evident from various expressions in his letters. Writing from London, in 1758, he says,—

"I also forgot, among the china, to mention a large fine jug for beer, to stand in the cooler. I fell in love with it at first sight; for I thought it looked like a fat jolly dame, clean and tidy, with a neat blue and white calico gown on, good natured and lovely, and put me in mind of—somebody."

This "somebody" appears again in some characteristic verses which the husband, not to be too chary of his poetic rhapsodies, read to the Junto as well as to his wife:

"Not a word of her face, of her shape, or her air,
    Or of flames, or of darts, you shall hear;
 I beauty admire, but virtue I prize,
    That fades not in seventy year.

"Am I loaded with care, she takes off a large share,
    That the burden ne'er makes me to reel;
 Does good fortune arrive, the joy of my wife
    Quite doubles the pleasure I feel.

"She defends my good name, even when I'm to blame,
    Firm friend as to man e'er was given;
 Her compassionate breast feels for all the distressed,
    Which draws down more blessings from heaven.
    *   *   *   *   *   *   *   *

"In peace and good order my household she guides,
    Right careful to save what I gain;
 Yet cheerfully spends, and smiles on the friends
    I've the pleasure to entertain.

12

" Some faults have we all, and so has my Joan,
    But then they're exceedingly small,
  And, now I'm grown used to them, so like my own
    I scarcely can see them at all."

There are no complaints or repinings
in Mrs. Franklin's letters to her husband,
which make her references to his absences
the more touching:

" Since you do so kindly inquire what things I want,
I will tell you that when Mrs. Franklin * came to town
and went to the assembly, Salley had nothing fit to
wear suitable to wait on her; and as I never should have
put on in your absence anything good, I gave Salley
my new robe as it wanted very little altering.   I should
be glad if you would bring me a plain satin gown," etc.

After explaining some household ar-
rangements, Mrs. Franklin exclaims, as
if the words had escaped her involun-
tarily, " O my child, there is great odds
between a man's being at home and
abroad; as everybody is afraid they shall
do wrong, so everything is left undone."
Making due allowance for the extrava-

---

* This was the wife of Governor Franklin, daughter-
in-law of Dr. Franklin, whose tablet in St. Paul's Church.
New York, records many virtues.

gance of the compliments which Mr. Black and Mr. Dunton were wont to lavish upon the fair sex, it is pleasant to learn from the former that the ladies of Annapolis and Philadelphia were as beautiful as the day, and adorned with all domestic charms, while we may believe that the Boston women possessed at least a portion of the graces with which Mr. Dunton endowed them. Of Mrs. Robert Breck, whom he designates as the "Flower of Boston," his "Chosen Exemplar of what a Widow is," he says,—

"Madam Brick is a Gentlewoman whofe Head (*i.e.* her Husband) has been cut off, and yet she lives and Walks: But don't be frighted, for she's Flefh and Blood ftill, and perhaps fome of the fineft that you ever faw. She has fufficiently evidenced that her Love to her late Husband is as strong as Death, becaufe Death has not been able to Extinguifh it."

After further extolling Madame Breck's high character, noble resignation, and beauty of person and carriage, which Mr. Dunton finds devoid of "the starch'dness usual amongst the Bostonians, who value themselves thereby so much, that they are

ready to say to all others, Stand off, for I
am holier than thou," he has the hardi-
hood to confess that all these virtues and
charms gave him

" so just a value for her that Mrs. Green wou'd often
say, Shou'd Iris Dye (which Heaven forbid) there's
none was fit to succeed her but Madam Brick ; But
Mrs. Green was partial, for my poor Pretences to secure
vertue, wou'd ne'er have answer'd to her Towring
heighths. 'Tis true, Madam Brick did me the Honour to
treat me very kindly at her House, and to admit me often
into her Converfation, but I am fure it was not on Love's,
but on Vertue's score.   For she well knows (at least as
well as I do) that Iris is alive :   And therefore I muft
justifie her Innocence on that account.   And tho' some
have been pleas'd to say, That were I in a fingle ftate,
they do believe she wou'd not be displeas'd with my
Addresses, As this is without any ground but groundlefs
Conjectures, so I hope I shall never be in a capacity to
make a Tryal of it." *

How Iris received these expressions the
journal does not relate.   There have been

* This lady, whose name Mr. Dunton persistently
wrote Brick, as it was pronounced, was the wife of ·
Robert Breck, of the same family as the well-known
Mr. Samuel Breck.   Mrs. Breck's noble resignation, for
which Mr. Dunton commends her, was further shown
by her taking to herself a second husband, Michael
Perry.

those who entertained the belief that Mr.
Dunton's mind was disturbed; but, although he often sails close to the wind,
he proves himself a good sailor by his
prudence in preparing for rocks and shoals
ahead, always prefacing his flattering remarks upon the beauties of Boston by
compliments to his wife, and assurances
that the same charms were found in her,
"as 'twere in a New Edition more Correct
and enlarged: Or rather, Iris is that
bright Original which all good Wives
ſhou'd imitate."

Although there were few who could
enter the lists with the incomparable
Madam Breck, Colonel Byrd has left, in
his diary of 1732, a characteristic sketch
of a charming Southern widow, Sarah
Syme, soon to become the wife of the
young Scotchman, John Henry, and the
mother of Patrick Henry:

"In the evening Tinsley conducted me to Mrs. Sym's
house, where I intended to take up my quarters. This
lady, at first suspecting that I was some lover, put on a
gravity that becomes a weed; but so soon as she learned
who I was, brightened up into an unusual cheerfulness

12*

and serenity. She was a portly, handsome dame, of
the family of Esau, and seemed not to pine too much
for the death of her husband, who was of the family of
the Saracens. This widow is a person of lively and
cheerful conversation, with much less reserve than most
of her countrywomen. It becomes her very well and
sets off her other agreeable qualities to advantage. We
tossed off a bottle of honest Port, which we relished
with a broiled chicken. At nine I retired to my de-
votions, and then slept so sound that fancy itself was
stupified, else I should have dreamed of my most
obliging landlady."

In addition to whatever "gift of tongues"
Patrick Henry may have derived from his
mother, he was, according to his latest
biographer, entitled to an inheritance of
eloquence upon his father's side, as his
paternal ancestry and Lord Brougham's
can be traced to a common stock.

When full and detailed letters and diaries have been preserved, as in the case of
the Winthrops, Pembertons, Morrises, Lo-
gans, Hopkinsons, Byrds, and others, we
realize our privileges and scan with interest the quaint pictures of the period, sympathizing with Mrs. James Pemberton when
she writes to her absent husband of the

British breaking into the plantation, burning her winter firewood, and trampling down her vegetable garden ; or entering into Mrs. Hopkinson's pleasure when her son Francis writes her of the cordial reception given him by his English relatives. Mrs. Hopkinson belonged to the Johnsons and Hydes, the latter Queen Anne's people, and Francis Hopkinson's letters from abroad are full of interesting details of life at Hartlebury Castle, the residence of his cousin the Bishop of Worcester, of English sayings and doings, and of encountering the Wests and other friends in London.

Mr. and Mrs. Benjamin West naturally entertained many Americans in their English home. Mr. Shewell, a cousin of Mrs. West, upon his return from England related numerous anecdotes of Mr. West's famous Sunday dinners, when Englishmen and distinguished countrymen of his own met around his hospitable board. " Mrs. West," he says, " was always American at heart, never losing her affection for her country and its customs. One day, while at dinner, a tall flunky placed a plate care-

fully covered with a napkin before Mrs.
West. 'Don't laugh at me, Cousin Tom!'
she exclaimed, lifting the napkin and re-
vealing a collection of corn-cobs. 'These
are the result of my endeavor to grow
green corn in our hot-house; but I had
the cobs boiled to get the smell, anyhow.'"

Mrs. West was a Philadelphia Quakeress,
as was her kinswoman, the mother of Leigh
Hunt. Of his mother's loveliness of character the poet writes with enthusiasm,
while Mrs. West seems to have possessed
a charm and vivacity all her own. A
painting by Benjamin West, recently discovered in a family garret, represents his
wife with her child in her arms, the costume and position evidently in imitation of
the old masters. West was an early patron
of the younger artist, John Singleton Copley, whose star, then rising, was destined
to eclipse that of his patron. A quaint
little sketch of Master Copley* and his

---

* This little boy was afterwards made Lord Lynd-
hurst, and was twice Lord Chancellor of England. His
daughter, the Hon. Sophia Copley, married Mr. Hamilton Beckett, thus uniting, after many years of residence

sister is to be found among West's draw-
ings, while the charming face of Mrs. Copley appears in a number of her husband's
paintings, especially in his Scriptural
scenes. Mrs. Copley, like Mrs. West,
was an ideal artist's wife, combining grace
and beauty with strong New England common sense and executive ability. To the
brush of Copley we are indebted for such interesting portraits of Colonial women as that
of the beautiful Lady Wentworth, in which
appears the flying squirrel, which seems to
have been as great a favorite with Copley
as was the King Charles spaniel with Van
Dyck; and that of Mrs. Samuel Alleyne
Otis, in the dress of a shepherdess, fair
enough to have won the heart of any
number of Florizels, and, like Perdita, to
have drawn her sheep to " leave grazing,
and only live by gazing."

Among Benjamin West's earlier portraits is that of Mrs. Thomas Hopkinson,
which now hangs in the rooms of the

---

abroad, these two distinguished American families, the
Hamiltons and the Copleys.

Historical Society of Pennsylvania, in the
company of her son and her son's son, the
latter, Joseph Hopkinson, author of " Hail
Columbia," surrounded by fair daughters and daughters-in-law. One of the
most attractive figures in this group is
Mary Hopkinson, wife of Dr. John Morgan. A lady in fanciful attire with a man-
dolin in her hand—the Hopkinsons were
then, as now, a musical race—is what the
painting reveals, while from her numerous letters we can form some idea of the
frank, observing, and vivacious young
woman, of whom her husband writes to
his mother-in-law in 1775, describing their
journey from Philadelphia to Cambridge,—

" Had Mrs. Morgan been a Princess she might have
been received with Pomp and Magnificence, but not
with a heartier welcome, were even her own Mamma,
the Queen Mother, to receive us, than our relations
have given us, both Mr. and Mrs. Clifford * and Mr.

---

* Probably Mr. and Mrs. Thomas Clifford, whose
country place, Rocky Point, on the Delaware, nearly
opposite Burlington, was so frequently visited by those
gay girls, the Misses Guest and Miss Sarah Eve. The
Misses Guest were nieces of Mrs. Clifford.

and Mrs. Kirkbride. She is an excellent companion at all times, but if possible excells herself on the road. She is full of spirits. Our horses are gentle as lambs and yet perform most admirably and we are truly happy that notwithstanding the rain, she escaped getting wet. It would delight you to get a glimpse of us just now, Col. Kirkbride at the violin and she at the harpsichord and sings most blithely and most sweetly."

Dr. John Morgan was appointed Director-General of Hospitals and Physician-in-Chief to the army in 1775, and it was upon this long and fatiguing journey that the husband and wife set forth so cheerfully. In one of her letters Mrs. Morgan begs her mother to write to her as often as possible, advising her to send her letters to Miss Morris, Mrs. Mifflin's sister, who had told her that "there would be an opportunity every three days." Of their reception at Cambridge she writes that there came

"six or eight of the gentlemen of the faculty to wait upon Dr. Morgan and escort us to the Camp, some of them on horse back and some of them in carriages. I do assure you we had no small cavalcade. My good friend Mrs. Mifflin met us on the way in her chariot and conducted us to her house, where we are to stay till we are settled in one of our own. You may, my dear

Mamma, depend upon hearing from me by every opportunity, and that very particularly but it must be a
private one for I do not intend to put you to expense of
postage.   Since I have begun this letter I have had the
honour of a visit from 4 Generals, Genl. Washington,
Gen. Putnam, Gen. Gates & Gen. Lee, while they were
here a very interesting scene happened.   There arrived an express of a Brig being taken belonging to the
enemy by one of our vessels, it is a valuable prize as it
was loaded with arms and ammunition, what delighted
me excessively was seeing the pleasure which shone in
every countenance particularly Gen. Gates's he was in
an ecstacy, and as Genl. Washington was reading the
invoice there was scarce an article that he did not com-
ment upon and that with so much warmth as diverted
everyone present."

Mrs. Morgan seems to have possessed
the happy faculty of extracting pleasure
and sweetness from all situations, consequently we find little or nothing in her
letters of the privations of her camp life
at Cambridge.

Mrs. John Adams speaks of calling
upon Mrs. Morgan, who, she says, " keeps
at Major Mifflin's," adding that she had
the pleasure of drinking coffee with Dr.
Morgan and his lady and the Major and
Mrs. Mifflin, " always having been an ad-

mirer of the latter and his delicate lady."
This visiting and paying of compliments,
and gossiping over dishes of tea and coffee
take us back into the heart of that old-
time life. Even the grim face of war is
sometimes made to present a holiday side,
as when the officers had a tea-drinking, or
when Mrs. Morgan witnessed a review of
the battalions. This last she describes
most graphically, even to giving the colors
of the different uniforms. Among others,
she speaks of a company composed entirely
of young Quakers, who were arrayed in a
light blue uniform turned up with white.
The "Light Infantry" she finds "as com-
pleat a company as can be, all gentlemen
and most of them young fellows and very
handsome, my neighbor Cadwalader Captain, and my brother, George Morgan, first
Lieutenant." Silas Deane's account of this
battalion of Associators, known as the
"Greens" and commanded by John Cadwalader, agrees with that of Mrs. Morgan.
He says that they wore green uniforms
faced with buff, their hat a hunter's cap,
and "were without exception the genteel-

est companies" he had ever seen.   Of the
Light Horse, later known as the Philadelphia City Troop, Mrs. Morgan writes,—

" Lastly come the 'Light Horse,' Mr. Markoe their
Captain—there is only five and twenty of them as yet
but really they look exceedingly well, you would be
surprised to see how well the horses are trained for the
little time they have exercised, in short they all did
exceedingly well and made a most martial appearance,
what did not a little inspire them was the presence of
a great number of the genteelest people of the place,
among whom was collected the most pretty girls I have
seen this long time."

" I shall not put off writing because I
happen not to be just as merry as a grig,"
says Mrs. Morgan to her sister.   Yet
through all her letters there runs a charming vein of vivacity and gayety of heart
which are in striking contrast to the sad
tone of a letter from Francis Hopkinson
to his brother-in-law, Dr. Samuel Coale,
of Baltimore, in which he tells him of the
death and burial of this much-loved sister.
" She was buried," he says, " under the
floor of St. Peter's Church near to the
remains of Mr. Duché's children.   The

morning was snowy and severely cold and
the walking very dangerous and slippery,
nevertheless a number of respectable citizens attended the funeral, and the pall was
borne by the first ladies of the place."

This custom of young girls and women
acting as pall-bearers is often alluded to in
journals of the day. When Mrs. Daniel
Phœnix, of New York, wife of the City
Treasurer, was buried, her pall-bearers were
women, and Miss Sarah Eve, in her diary,
written in Philadelphia in 1772 and '73,
remarks in her usual independent and vivacious manner, " B. Rush, P. Dunn, K.
Vaughan and myself carried Mr. Ash's
child to be buried; foolish custom for
Girls to prance it through the streets without hats or bonnets!"* Miss Eve says nothing about wearing a veil, although we read

---

* A curious incident is, that while reading the above,
in 1890, a brother of the child buried in 1772, Mr.
John Morgan Ash, came into the rooms of the Historical Society of Pennsylvania. To give authority to this
statement, it may be well to explain that the father of
this sister and brother of such different ages—Colonel
Ash, of the Revolution—was born in 1750, was married

elsewhere of the girl pall-bearers being dressed in white and wearing long white veils, as at the funeral of Fanny Durdin in 1812.

Occasionally, as if to prove to us that our dear grandmothers enjoyed themselves, girlish laughter and frolic illuminate the pages of some old record, and we read of merry-makings or love-makings that beguiled the passing hour, as when young Mr. Porter's best man stole away his fair bride, Elizabeth Pitkin, or from a letter of Mrs. Edward Carrington, of Virginia, learn how her sister, Mary Ambler, captivated the learned Chief-Justice Marshall, whose wife she afterwards became.

"Our expectations were raised to the highest pitch, and the little circle of York was on tiptoe on his arrival. Our girls particularly, were emulous who should be the first introduced; it is remarkable that my sister, then only *fourteen* and diffident beyond all others, de-

---

three times, and had twenty-four children. The baby which Miss Eve helped to carry to its grave in 1772 was born when Colonel Ash was twenty or twenty-one, while Mr. John Morgan Ash, a child of the third marriage, was born early in the present century.

clared that we were giving ourselves useless trouble,
for that she, for the first time, had made up her mind to
go to the ball (though she had not even been to dancing-
school), and was resolved to set her cap at him and
eclipse us all.   This in the end proved true, and at the
first introduction he became devoted to her."

In the diary of Lucinda of Virginia,
who writes to her dear Marcia from " Bush-
field" and " The Wilderness," we hear of
country visits, tea-drinkings, and all the
pleasant sociability that belonged to life in
the Old Dominion.   She wept over " Lady
Julia Mandeville," this tender-hearted Lucinda, until her eyes were so red that
she was ashamed to see her beaux, and
then, although she had " but little time
to smart herself," she " craped" her hair,
put on a " Great-Coat," and considered
herself " drest."   She tells Marcia that
one evening she and Milly Washington
were " minded to eat" after they had
decorously retired to their rooms for the
night, and, having taxed their digestions
with a dish of bacon and beef, followed
by a bowl of sago cream, were about
to enter upon the delights of a nocturnal
" apple pye," when Mr. Corbin Washing-

ton, in his wife's short gown and petticoat, and Mrs. Washington, in her husband's coat, burst in upon the scene and gave the youthful revellers a fine fright, after which they all settled down to enjoy the "apple pye" together.   Elsewhere the same chronicler tells of Mr. Newton having received "his discard" from her cousin Nancy, and, with never a regret for the disappointed lover, gleefully relates that he could not tell the difference between "The Belle's Stratagem" and "The Country Cousin" when read in the distracting presence of Miss Nancy.   They were sad coquettes in their youth, these fair dames, although they look so demure in their portraits, and proved such exemplary wives and mothers in later years.   Duels and despairing lovers seem scarcely to have ruffled the serenity of their lovely countenances, or to have made their hearts beat faster under their stiff bodices.   Did they realize, with a wisdom beyond their years, that heart-breaks were not of necessity fatal ?   Yet how crushed and bruised the poor hearts seemed !

Thomas Jefferson, at the age of nineteen, filled his letters to his friend, John Page, with rhapsodies upon the form and face of his " Belinda," humbly prays for another watch paper cut by her hands, and calls upon Providence to sustain him through the trial should she refuse him at the next Apollo ball, where he designs putting his fate to the touch.   That he lost we know, as Rebecca Burwell, his " Belinda," soon after became the wife of Jacqueline Ambler, of Virginia ; and although Jefferson felt, poor lad, that from him the joys of life had fled forever, it was not long before he recovered and became the devoted lover of Martha Skelton, who made Monticello an earthly paradise to her young husband during the brief period of their married life.   Another beautiful Miss Burwell, also of Williamsburg, turned the head of an earlier Virginia statesman, Francis Nicholson, who, like an Eastern sultan rather than a Colonial governor, proposed to cut the throats of his rival, of the clergyman who performed the ceremony, and of the justice who issued the license.

" C'est l'amour, c'est l'amour
Qui tourne le monde ronde !"

It seems as if the old couplet had been
singing itself down all the years to assure
us that these grandmothers and grand-
fathers of ours, with all their wisdom and
sacrifice and devotion to duty, were capable of the same endearing follies that belong to their children of to-day.

Gage's Headquarters.

OLD LANDMARKS.

TREADING the stone floors of old Christ
Church, Philadelphia, under which lie
buried early governors of Pennsylvania
and soldiers of Colonial times, we can picture to ourselves President Washington,
stately little Lady Washington, and lovely
Nellie Custis, preceded by their footman,
entering the church to take their places in
the pew reserved for them between those
of Bishop White and Dr. Franklin. Sitting in the Washington pew, in Christ

Church at Alexandria, where the General was a vestryman, the spare form and intellectual face of the present rector under the sounding-board recall Seba Smith's lines,—

> " That sounding board, to me it seemed
>   A cherub poised on high—
> A mystery I almost deemed
>   Quite hid from vulgar eye ;
> And that old pastor, wrapt in prayer,
> Looked doubly awful 'neath it there."

In Trinity Church, New York, once called King's Chapel, the tombs and memorials of early American bishops and heroes almost cause us to overlook the fact that but one stone remains of the original building ; while in the older church of St. Paul's, one remembers that William Vesey, reared upon the stern doctrine of Increase Mather, turned aside from that especial way of righteousness to preach here as early as 1704.   Farther north, in a region long inhospitable to churches, Cotton Mather having announced that he " found no just ground in Scripture to apply such a trope as church to a public assembly," we find our way through the winding streets of old

Salem to the first meeting-house, erected
in 1634, only two years after that of Smith-
field, Virginia.   As severe and unadorned
in its architecture as the religious life of
its founders is this little building, which
proclaims with a certain force the doctrine
for which they contended,—the right of
man to seek his God and serve Him according to the dictates of his conscience.
We turn from Boston's " Old South," long
the stronghold of Puritanism, to Christ
Church, called the " Old North," from
which the signal lantern was hung aloft in
the belfry arch on the night of April 18,
1775 ; or, wandering through the aisles of
King's Chapel, pause before the governor's
pew to remember that General Washington
worshipped here long before the Revolution,* or notice the square pew, once
adorned with the royal arms of England,

---

* Colonel Washington went to Boston in 1756, accompanied by Captain George Mercer, to confer with
General Shirley with reference to the precedence in
military rank between crown and provincial commis-
sions.—" Early Sketches of George Washington," by
William S. Baker.

which was in Colonial days reserved for
any member of the Hanover family who
might be pleased to cross the water to visit
his American subjects. Worshipping to-
day in such ancient churches as are left to
this generation, or reading familiar names
from the tablets upon their walls, or from
the headstones in their graveyards, that
old life seems so near our own, so knit to
it by strands of religious faith and domestic association, that we can almost see the
stately throng of men and women as they
once passed through the doors and along
the aisles to their pews. The ladies are
stiff in satin, brocade and buckram, and
yet not too rigid to send forth bewilder-
ing glances from beneath their overshad-
owing plumed hats upon the cavaliers who
attend them, and who are as brave as they
in their picturesque costumes, rich with
lace and embroidery. Even in New England, with all the preaching and legislating
against silk, lace, embroideries, cut-works,
and slashed garments, human nature prevailed. The Abbé Robin remarked, in
view of the gaudy dress of the women in

church, that it was the only theatre that they had for the display of their finery, while we with equal indulgence may pardon those fair ones of the olden time who allowed their eyes to wander in the pauses of devotion toward the Governor's pew where Madam, recently returned from a visit to her English relatives, was seated, resplendent in the latest London modes.

Mr. Bynner has given us a picture of the first appearance of Agnes Surriage and Sir Henry Frankland at church together, the occasion being the funeral service of Madam Shirley, the kindly and generous friend of the fisherman's daughter from Marblehead. Induced to appear in public with her lover through her strong affection for her benefactress, Agnes, in deep mourning, takes her place in a pew near that of the governor and his children, where she is soon made to feel the bitter scorn of the high-born dames who had once delighted to heap compliments upon her beauty, while Sir Henry finds that he is powerless to defend the shrinking girl from the insolent glances of his comrades. These

14

picturesque figures in the quaint setting of
King's Chapel form a striking and impres-
sive scene worthy of the pen which has
portrayed it for this generation.   Near
Christ Church is still shown the house at
the corner of Tileston Street, where Agnes
dwelt under the roof of the austere widow,
and where she tended the little garden
which, from its luxuriant growth of rare
flowers and plants, was the wonder of the
neighborhood.

Strolling through another and far more
spacious garden upon the banks of the Potomac, whose box-bordered beds and trim
parterres tell of the French gardener who
laid out the grounds of Mount Vernon, or
standing upon the high bluff, where Washington must often have stood to enjoy the
lovely sweep of the shining river, we can
form some idea of the beauty and·seclusion
that surrounded the home life of the stately
but simple-hearted Virginia gentleman and
gentlewoman.   "There," says the gardener, "are some fine tulip- and ash-trees
planted by the General, here are some
hydrangeas that the Marquis de Lafayette

brought with him in 1824, and here is the rose-bush beside which Lawrence Lewis proposed to Nellie Custis," adding, " The negroes call it the magic rose, as it is supposed to insure the success of the most unpromising love-affair."

Such associations bring the old life before us with a sudden crowding upon the canvas of historic scenes and figures. The long, low house, elegant with all its simplicity, covered less ground in Colonial times than it now does. In early days it was the home of Captain Lawrence Washington, who named his Virginia plantation after Admiral Vernon, under whom he had served in the English expedition against Cartagena, and for whom he ever entertained a warm friendship. A painting of Admiral Vernon before Cartagena, given to Lawrence Washington by the admiral in recognition of this friendship, is still hanging over one of the mantels of Mount Vernon, where is also a portrait of the handsome, dark-eyed owner of the estate. Its mistress, in those days, was Anne, daughter of the Hon. William Fairfax, who

occupied the position of collector of customs in Salem and Marblehead before he
came to Belvoir, Virginia, to become president of the Council of that State. Mrs.
Washington, the mother of George and
the step-mother of Lawrence, is now at
Mount Vernon more frequently, perchance,
than under its later mistress, there having
existed a friendship of long standing, if
not a family connection, between the
Washingtons and the Fairfaxes. George
is coming and going, like a child of the
house, between his long surveying expedi-
tions for Lord Fairfax in the western wilds,
where, if there were often no knives upon
the table " to eat with," there seems always
to have been a pen with which to record
the experiences of the day. A great favorite with the owner of Mount Vernon,
and destined to be his heir, is the tall strip-
ling, whose face and form give promise of
the distinguished presence that was later
to command respect at home and abroad.
Something strangely interesting there is
in all that relates to the youth of Washington, whether in his mother's home, or

at Mount Vernon, or as the welcome guest
of old Lord Fairfax at Greenway Court in
the Shenandoah Valley.

Although heavy responsibilities were
placed upon these young shoulders, it is
pleasant to know that Washington often
joined in fox-hunts, a favorite pastime of
the Virginia gentry, and also that he was
as capable of "sighing like a furnace" as
any other love-struck swain. At seventeen he wrote to his "dear Friend Robin,"
from Belvoir,

"I might, was my heart disengag'd, pass my time
very pleasantly as there's a very agreeable Young Lady
Lives in the same house (Col⁰ George Fairfax's Wife's
Sister) but as thats only adding Fuel to fire it makes
me more uneasy for by often and unavoidably being in
Company with her revives my former Passion for your
Low Land Beauty whereas was I to live more retired
from Young Women I might in some measure eliviate
my sorrows by burying that chast and troublesome Passion in the grave of oblivion or eternall forgetfulness,
. . . as I am well convinced was I ever to attempt
any thing I should only get a denial which would be
only adding grief to uneasiness."

The modesty of this effusion certainly
adds to its attractiveness; and as for the

spelling—vowels and consonants seem, in those days, to have been used in hap-hazard fashion by older writers than those of seventeen years. That Washington could not have mourned very long over this " chast and troublesome Passion," whose object is supposed to have been Miss Lucy Grymes, afterwards the mother of General Henry Lee, is evident from the fact that he was beginning to find " the Young Lady in the house," Miss Mary Cary, very agreeable ; while that he did not practise his theory of living " retired from Young Women" is proved by subsequent experiences.

A New York house that naturally links itself in thought with Mount Vernon is the old Philipse Manor, where Mary Philipse spent her early days. Here the Philipses presided for generations over vast estates in the counties of Westchester, Dutchess, and Putnam, being known among their tenantry as the Junkers (pronounced Yonkers), or gentlemen *par excellence*, to which title the town of Yonkers, that gradually grew up around the old manor-house, owes its name.

This was the home of her childhood, but it was at the house of her sister, Mrs. Beverly Robinson, that Mary Philipse met Colonel Washington. The history of this rather shadowy love-affair has never been fully told, although frequently referred to. Mr. Irving's explanation is that the young soldier, ever alert in the path of duty, quitted too soon the lists of love for those of war, thus leaving the field to his rival, Colonel Morris. In support of this theory, Mr. Irving remarks upon the great despatch with which Washington conducted his wooing of the widow Custis, soon after, as if " he feared, should he leave the matter in suspense, some more enterprising rival might supplant him during his absence, as in the case of Miss Philipse, at New York." With due respect to Mr. Irving, it does not seem consistent with the character of Washington to turn aside so readily from the pursuit of anything that he greatly desired ; and from the fact that Miss Philipse so soon after married Colonel Morris, it is more natural to conclude that her affections were engaged

before she met the young Virginian. There
being no positive data on the subject, and
the spirit of a love-affair being about as
difficult to transmit from one generation
to another as the tone of a voice or the
glance of an eye, we feel free to put upon
the affair the construction that detracts
least from the dignity of the American
hero. After her marriage, Mary Philipse
lived in the home which Colonel Morris
built upon a high bank of the Harlem
River, about a mile from the site of old
Fort Washington, one of the most picturesque spots upon the island. This
house, still standing and in good preservation, a fine example of a Colonial residence, was long known as the Roger Morris and later as the Jumel House. The
best view of the mansion is to be had from
the river-drive near One Hundred and
Sixty-First Street, while from the portico
there is a fine prospect of the Harlem River
and of the great city which has grown up
around it since its erection in 1758. Strange
to relate, Washington made his head-quarters here while engaged in military opera-

tions around New York in the autumn of
1776, and barely escaped capture in the
home of his former friends, as the British
troops took possession of the premises a
half-hour after the American General had
vacated them. Here also General Knyp-
hausen, unused to such surroundings, if we
are to believe the strange tales told of his
spreading the butter on his bread with his
fingers, and of other eccentricities at table,
had his head-quarters during the British
occupation of New York.

At the close of the war the property of
Colonel Morris was confiscated and the
house was for a time an inn, where parties from New York were entertained.
Once again General (then President) Washington visited the old mansion, as he records in his diary of July 10, 1790:

" Having formed a Party consisting of the Vice-
President [John Adams], his lady and Son and Miss
Smith, the Secretaries of State, Treasury and War
[Thomas Jefferson, Alexander Hamilton, and General
Knox] and the ladies of the two latter, with all the
gentlemen of my family, Mrs. Lear and the two chil-
dren, we visited the old position of Fort Washington,
and afterwards dined on a dinner provided by Mr.

Mariner, at the house lately of Colonel Morris, but confiscated and in the possession of a common Farmer."

The house later passed into the hands
of Stephen Jumel, who with his wife, gay
Madame Jumel, lived here in great state
and luxury, driving their carriage drawn
by eight horses, and giving entertainments
as celebrated for their sumptuousness and
luxury as were those of Madam Rush
of Philadelphia at a later date.   Here
Stephen Jumel died, and here occurred that
strangest of weddings, when Aaron Burr,
refused again and again by Madame Jumel, appeared at her door one day, accompanied by the Rev. Dr. Bogart, and
insisted upon marrying her. Why the lady
consented it is difficult to discover, unless
Aaron Burr at seventy-eight still retained
some of the attractions that had rendered
him irresistible at an earlier age.   Upon
one occasion, at her own home, Colonel
Burr had, in handing Madame Jumel in to
dinner, said, " I give you my hand, madame ; my heart has long been yours."

The guests probably looked upon the

expressions of the elderly man of fashion as withered flowers of speech natural to one who had passed his youth in an age of extravagant compliment, and great surprise was expressed by the friends of Madame Jumel when it became known that she had yielded to the importunities of her aged suitor, especially when they learned of the out-of-hand manner in which the affair had been conducted. Somewhat similar to this is a story told of Colonel Nathaniel Burwell, of Carter Hall, Virginia, who was so afflicted by the death of his wife, Susanna Grymes, that he went to Rosewell and requested Governor John Page to send for his young and beautiful, widowed half-sister, Mrs. George W. Baylor, for him to marry. The widow came obedient to the summons, but objected, upon which Colonel Burwell exclaimed, "Lucy, you don't know what is good for you; your brother John and I arranged it all before you came," which dogmatic assertion seeming to satisfy Mrs. Baylor, she acceded to the family arrangement with the meekness of a woman of the Old Testament. After the ceremony, the groom, turning to the fair bride, said, " Now, Lucy, you can weep for your dear George and I will weep for my beloved Suky !"

We are not told that Colonel Burr and Madame Jumel spent their days in weeping over their respective consorts; but there is good authority for believing that tears were shed by one at least of this ill-assorted couple.

Another picture remains of a scene in the old mansion, when Madame Jumel was entertaining Joseph Bonaparte. Madame refused to pass through the door to take her place at table in advance of her guest, because he was a prince. The gentleman bowed and politely declined to take precedence of a lady, while the guests stood aside, waiting to see how the question of etiquette would be decided. How the matter was settled upon this occasion is not related, but two doors cut through later, and still standing side by side, show how the hostess avoided similar complications in the future.

The *bouweries* of Governor Stuyvesant,

Stephen Van Cortlandt, and Jacobus Kip
were in what is now the heart of the great
city, the possessions of the influential families of De Lancey and Roosevelt were
in the centre of the island, while farther
up the Hudson were the vast manors of
the Beekmans, Livingstons, Van Rens-
selaers, Schuylers, and Johnsons, where
these patroons lived among and ruled
over their tenantry like the feudal lords
of old England. When a member of the
Van Rensselaer family died, the tenants,
sometimes amounting to several thousand, says Bishop Kip, came down to
Albany to pay their respects to his memory, and to drink to the peace of his soul
in good ale from his generous cellars.
The cannon which stood at the entrance
of the Van Rensselaer manor-house, and
which was always fired upon the birth or
death of one of the family, is still preserved
to testify to the honors paid these long
dead and gone patroons. The burial of
Philip Livingston, in 1749, upon which occasion services were performed at his house
in New York as well as at the manor-

H 15

house, is thus described in a journal of the day :

"In the city, the lower rooms of most of the houses in Broadstreet, where he resided, were thrown open to receive visitors. A pipe of wine was spiced for the occasion, and to each of the eight bearers, with a pair of gloves, mourning ring, scarf and handkerchief, a *monkey-spoon* was given. [This was so called from the figure of an ape or monkey which was carved *in solido* at the extremity of the handle. It differed from a common spoon in having a circular and very shallow bowl.] At the manor these ceremonies were all repeated, another pipe of wine was spiced, and besides the same presents to the bearers, a pair of black gloves and a handkerchief were given to each of the tenants. The whole expense was said to amount to £500."*

Many interesting associations cluster round the Livingston manor, built by Chancellor Livingston. The old homestead of Judge Robert R. Livingston and his wife, Margaret Beekman, was destroyed by the British in 1777. From this happy home, to whose mistress Judge Livingston

---

* At funerals in old New York it was customary to serve hot wine in winter and sangaree in summer. Burnt wine was sometimes served in silver tankards.— " History of New York," by William L. Stone.

writes after thirteen years of married life,
" My imagination paints you with all your
loveliness, with all the charms my soul has
so many years doated on," came such sons
as Robert R. Livingston, first Chancellor
of the State of New York, Colonel Henry
B. Livingston, and youngest, but not least
important, Edward, the distinguished lawyer and statesman, who married the beautiful widow Moreau. Janet Livingston
married General Montgomery, who fell at
Quebec, while her youger sister, Alida, became the wife of General John Armstrong.
Robert R. Livingston represented the
United States at the Court of France, and,
although very deaf, was as fluent and entertaining in French as in English. He was
succeeded by his brother-in-law, General
Armstrong, who could speak no French,
upon which Napoleon exclaimed, " What
strange people are these Americans ! First
they send me a deaf man, and then one
who is dumb."

In New Jersey, Pennsylvania, and Delaware, where the patroon system did not
prevail, there were extensive manors laid

out for the Biddles, Norrises, Penns, and
others, and handsome mansions, as that at
Belmont where William Peters and his
wife, Mary Brientnal, lived before the
Revolution, and where their son, the
learned and witty Judge Peters, resided
later; The Hills, once a McPherson property, to which General Arnold took his
lovely bride, Margaret Shippen, in the
summer of 1779; and Lansdowne, the
country-seat of John Penn, where, in days
after the Revolution, the beautiful Mrs.
Bingham held a court worthy of a princess.

Mr. Breck tells an amusing story of
Mrs. Bingham's attempt to introduce the
foreign fashion of having her guests announced. "The doctor and Miss Peggy"
were the names given by the unsuspect-
ing coachman to the servant in livery,
who, with the literalness that seems to
belong to the liveried official, repeated
"The doctor and Miss Peggy" to the next
lackey, and thus the names were sounded
through the great halls to the drawing-
room, where "the doctor and Miss Peggy,"
Dr. Kuhn and his step-daughter, Miss

Markoe, arrived in a state of rather un-
dignified merriment.

South of Lansdowne is Woodlands, still
standing, a good example of a handsome
Colonial mansion. Here lived Andrew
Hamilton, known all through the Colonies
as a great lawyer, having won the celebrated Zenger case in New York, which,
like that of John Wilkes in England, resolved itself into a sturdy Anglo-Saxon
protest against restricting the liberty of the
press,—such liberty as we now possess, and
in whose exercise we sometimes feel as did
the Israelites of old, that the desire of our
hearts has been granted, but that leanness
has entered into our souls. In a London
letter to the *Pennsylvania Gazette*, Mr.
Hamilton is spoken of as a "Goliath in
Learning and Politics," while great English
barristers admitted that the subject of libels
had never been so well treated at West-
minster Hall as in New York by Andrew
Hamilton, which shows that the proverbial
Philadelphia lawyer was abroad at an early
day. It was the second Andrew Hamilton who was living at Woodlands when

15*

Mr. Black came to Philadelphia, and who, with Secretary Peters and Mr. Robert Strettell, welcomed him into the Province with old-time hospitality and "a Bowl of fine Lemon Punch big enough to have Swimm'd half a dozen of young geese." Near Woodlands, overlooking the river, is the house of John Bartram, surrounded by his famous botanical garden, the first in the country. Some of the trees are still standing under which sat such great scientists as Dr. Casper Wistar, Dr. Rush, and David Rittenhouse, or such statesmen as Jefferson and Adams.

Wakefield, a Fisher homestead, and James Logan's residence, Stenton, to which the friendly Indians came in such numbers that they were obliged to encamp upon the lawn, are both in the Germantown neighborhood; while to walk along the narrow Main Street is like taking a journey into the past century, so many sober, drab-colored façades and charming white-columned doors present themselves, offering dignified rebuke to the noisy, modern trolley that whirls between them.

Notable among the older and more spacious dwellings is Cliveden, the Chew house, which appears in Revolutionary prints emitting flame and smoke, like the dragons of fairy lore, with riflemen firing from every window and armed Continentals charging across its lawn. As the home of Councillor Benjamin Chew and his bevy of gay daughters, this house has a history of its own, before the war and after; and during the British occupation Major André was often there. A pleasant picture of these days at Cliveden has lately come to us from a member of the family, with some verses written by André upon seeing Miss Peggy's fair face framed by a spray of apple-blossoms. Love and hope were in their spring-time with this pair, and who can tell what vows were exchanged beneath the blossoming branches of the Cliveden trees, especially as later disclosures seem to place almost beyond question the report that the young officer was engaged to Miss Chew, whose knight he was in the famous Meschianza? That Peggy Chew did not marry until seven

years after André's death is a rather significant fact in view of her attractions and
the early age at which women married in
those days.   Her marriage to General
Howard, the hero of Cowpens, was solemnized in the Chew house on Third
Street, upon which occasion Washington
was present and doubtless trod a measure,
as the Commander-in-Chief had a warm admiration for this family of bright sisters, with
whose father he was upon friendly terms.*

Mrs. Sophie Howard Ward says that
after her grandmother's marriage she
still loved to dwell upon Major André's
charms, while her patriotic husband was
wont to cut short her reminiscences by
exclaiming, "He was a —— spy, nothing
but a —— spy!"

Beautiful with the serene beauty of old

---

* Although obliged to leave Philadelphia in August,
1777, being under arrest as an officer of the Crown,
Mr. Chew was allowed to come back to his home in
May, 1778, no overt act being charged against him.
Later, under the new government, he was Judge and
President of the High Court of Excise and Appeals of
Pennsylvania from 1791 until 1808.

age, rich with many associations clustered about it, stands the Wister homestead, Grumblethorpe. Built by John Wister, who came to Pennsylvania in 1727, this was the first summer residence erected by a Philadelphian in Germantown. Vernon, another Wister house, is much more picturesquely situated upon what was once the property of Melchior Meng. Although Grumblethorpe stands directly upon the Main Street, the garden and grounds reach back some distance, embracing several acres, and boasting a charming garden full of old-fashioned flowers, and a pear-tree planted by John Wister, the first settler. One of the *habitués* of this house was Count Zinzendorf, a man of high rank and large possessions, who came to America in the interests of the Moravian Church. The Saxon nobleman was an intimate friend of Mr. Wister's, who, in his later years, strongly inclined towards the religion of the Hussites.

In this mansion, long known as the "Wister's Big House," General Agnew made his head-quarters, and hither, after

m

the battle of Germantown, he was carried mortally wounded. The spot is still shown where he died; the blood-stains are upon the floor, like those at Holyrood which tell where Rizzio fell. Under the spell of the associations of that older time, we read, over the gallant officer's signature, tender, manly words written to his wife, telling her that the war will not last many months, when it will be his pleasure to dedicate to her the rest of his life; and, quite forgetting that he was our country's enemy, we think of him only as a brave gentleman who died in a strange land in the honest discharge of his duty. War seems terrible—a ghastly spectre divested of all pomp and circumstance—when we think of Agnew dying of his wounds in the old Germantown house, far from his Mary and the children whom he loved, or hear the words of a British officer to his men who were burying the dead from the field of Germantown, "Don't bury them with their faces up, and thus cast dirt in their faces. They are all mothers' sons."

Wedding bells were heard in the old home as well as funeral dirges. Here, under the moulded circle in the parlor ceiling, Major Lennox, an American officer who had his head-quarters in the Wister house, was married to Miss Lukens, who, like a heroine of romance, spent her honeymoon in this beleaguered castle. Passing from the parlor into the hall, we are suddenly confronted with a life-size figure of a British grenadier in full uniform, who stands here like a sentinel guarding the memorials of the past. This wooden figure, which is admirable in outline and coloring, has been attributed to Major André; but the fact that it plays a prominent part in Sally Wister's diary of life in the Foulke house, at Penllyn, where the Wister family took refuge before the battle of Germantown, precludes this idea. André's scenery and drops for the little theatre in Southwark were painted several months later, and Miss Wister herself says, "We had brought some weeks ago a British grenadier from Uncle Miles's on purpose to divert us." The young girl's

description of the pranks played with this
soldier of wood and paint, written for the
entertainment of her friend Miss Deborah
Norris, has the freshness and vivacity of
a story of to-day. It had been planned
by the " amiable Major Stodard" and her
mischievous self to give poor Mr. Tilly a
fright. After explaining that the British
grenadier had been placed near a door
opening into the road, another figure
near by "to add to the deceit," Miss
Wister relates the success of her rather
severe practical joke:

" Sixth Day, Night.

" In the beginning of the evening I went to Liddy
and beg'd her to secure the swords and pistols which
were in their parlour. The Marylander, hearing our
voices, joined us. I told him of our proposal. Whether
he thought it a good one or not I can't say, but he ap-
prov'd of it, and Liddy went in and brought her apron
full of swords and pistols. When this was done, Stodard join'd the officers. We girls went and stood at the
first landing of the stairs. The gentlemen were very
merry, and chatting on public affairs, when Seaton's
negro (observe that Seaton, being indisposed, was ap-
priz'd of the scheme) open'd the door, candle in hand,
and said, ' There's somebody at the door that wishes to
see you.' ' Who? All of us?' said Tilly. ' Yes, Sir,'

said the boy. They all rose (the Major, as he said afterwards, almost dying with laughter), and walked into the entry, Tilly first, in full expectation of news. The first object that struck his view was a British sol- dier. In a moment his ears were saluted, ' Is there any rebel officers here ?' in a thundering voice. Not waiting for a second word, he darted like lightning out of the front door, through the yard, bolted o'er the fence. Swamps, fences, thorn-hedges and plough'd fields no way impeded his retreat. He was soon out of hearing. The woods echoed with, ' Which way did he go? Stop him! Surround the house!' The amiable Lips- comb had his hand on the latch of the door, intending to make his escape; Stodard, considering his indisposi- tion, acquainted him with the deceit. We females ran down stairs to join in the general laugh. I walked into Jesse's parlour. There sat poor Stodard (whose sore lips must have receiv'd no advantage from this), almost convuls'd with laughing, rolling in an arm-chair. He said nothing; I believe he could not have spoke. ' Major Stodard,' said I, 'go to call Tilly back. He will lose himself,—indeed he will;' every word inter rupted with a ' Ha! ha!' At last he rose, and went to the door; and what a loud voice could avail in bringing him back, he tried. Figure to thyself this Tilly, of a snowy evening, no hat, shoes down at the heel, hair unty'd, flying across meadows, creeks, and mud-holes. Flying from what? Why, a bit of painted wood. But he was ignorant of what it was. The idea of being made a prisoner wholly engrossed his mind, and his last resource was to run.

"After a while, we being in more composure, and

our bursts of laughter less frequent, yet by no means
subsided,—in full assembly of girls and officers,—Tilly
enter'd.   The greatest part of my risibility turn'd to
pity.   Inexpressible confusion had taken entire possession of his countenance, his fine hair hanging dishevell'd
down his shoulders, all splashed with mud; yet his
bright confusion and race had not divested him of his
beauty.   He smil'd as he trip'd up the steps; but 'twas
vexation plac'd it on his features.   Joy at that moment
was banished from his heart.   He briskly walked five
or six steps, then stop'd, and took a general survey of
us all.   'Where *have* you been, Mr. Tilly?' ask'd one
officer.   (We girls were silent.)   'I really imagin'd,'
said Major Stodard, 'that you were gone for your pistols, I follow'd you to prevent danger,'—an excessive
laugh at each question, which it was impossible to re-
strain.   'Pray, where were your pistols, Tilly?'   He
broke his silence by the following expression: 'You
may all go to the D—l.'   I never heard him utter an
indecent expression before."

That this adventure was rather discom-
fiting to Mr. Tilly may be gathered from
the smart journalizer's statement that on
First day night he had not " said a sylla-
ble to one of us young ladies since Sixth
day eve."   When the silence was finally
broken, Mr. Tilly showed that all bitterness
had departed from his soul, as he yielded
to the good-natured merriment of the hour

and gave the company a humorous account of his own exploits.

Between Germantown and Philadelphia was Fair Hill, the home of Isaac Norris, and near Frankford, upon a fair green spot in the midst of a net-work of railroads, stands Chalkley Hall. Of this country-seat and its former owner, the devout visiting Friend, Thomas Chalkley, the poet Whittier wrote after a stroll through the grounds,—

" Beneath the arms
Of this embracing wood, a good man made
His home, like Abraham resting in the shade
Of Mamre's lonely palms."

The old mansion, which has been in the possession of the Wetherill family since 1817, was long the home of Abel James, who married a daughter of Thomas Chalkley. Tradition tells of a great dinner given here in Colonial days, when eighty covers were laid, and the soup was served to each guest in a silver porringer. The hall of the old house is spacious enough to admit of an even larger company; but the story

of the eighty porringers is a trifle problem-
atical, although that some such articles of
plate existed members of the family are
able to prove by the most conclusive of all
demonstrations.   Another famous dinner,
spread by Mrs. Abel James, in 1777, for
some ill-fed Continental soldiers encamped
in the neighborhood, was unceremoniously
interrupted by the sentry's cry, " The Red-
coats are upon us !"   A sudden shifting
of figures upon the scene ensued, the invited guests retreating by one door, while
the unbidden convives entered by the
other, and, taking their places at the board,
fell with a will upon Mrs. James's good
cheer, for which they afterwards had the
grace to thank her most politely.   Another story told of this kindly mistress of
Chalkley Hall is, that during the British
occupation she frequently carried a little
pig under the seat of her chaise to some
of her friends in Philadelphia who were
greatly in need of food.   The dignified
Quaker lady passed the British sentinel
unmolested, no person suspecting her of
smuggling live-stock through the lines.

Hearing an old Philadelphian recount his boyish exploits upon the cherry-trees of his neighbor Charles Wharton and describe in detail his and other fine old homes on Second Street, we can form some idea of the spaciousness of these dwellings, with their terraced gardens in the rear reaching back to Third Street, and capacious cellars in which were stored hogsheads of rum from Jamaica and casks of wine from Lisbon and the Canaries. John Cadwalader built a house on Second Street prior to 1774, as John Adams and Silas Deane both wrote of being dined and wined here at that date. The latter says, "I dined yesterday with Mr. Cadwalader, whose furniture and house exceed anything I have seen in this city or elsewhere." It was in his large garden, reaching to Third Street, that John Cadwalader drilled and entertained in great style the military company raised by him, the first formed in Pennsylvania. This company, "the Greens," called in derision the "Silk Stocking Company," most of its members being gentlemen, afterwards formed a part of General

Cadwalader's brigade, which distinguished itself upon many battle-fields.

Over this home on Second Street presided Elizabeth Lloyd, the first wife of General Cadwalader, and, later, beautiful Williamina Bond, and here grew into the loveliness that afterwards distinguished them such fair daughters of the house as Maria Cadwalader, who married General Samuel Ringgold, of Fountain Rock, Maryland, and Frances, who became the wife of David Montagu Erskine, sometime secretary to the British legation in Philadelphia.*   A miniature of Frances

---

* A daughter of Lord and Lady Erskine married James Henry Callender, and was celebrated for her beauty in England and on the Continent. Another daughter, the Hon. Mary Erskine, married, in 1832, Hermann, Count von Baumgarten, of Bavaria. A story has prevailed, and even found its way into print, that this English lady was the author of " The Initials," " Quits," etc. To correct this *on-dit* it is only necessary to state that Mary Erskine, Countess von Baumgarten, died March 15, 1874, while the author of " The Initials" died November 12, 1893. The latter was Jemima, daughter of James Montgomery, of Sea View, County Donegal, of the branch of the noble house of the Montgomerys of Eglinton, that has long been settled in the

Cadwalader, painted after she became Lady Erskine, was sent from England to her cousin, Mrs. Samuel Blodget. The portraits of the two kinswomen show that they inherited no small share of the beauty of their ancestress, Williamina Moore, of Moore Hall.

Not far from the Cadwaladers', at the corner of Second and Union Streets, Archibald McCall, the India merchant, built a home about 1762, which is still standing. In its great garden were kept various animals, brought from foreign parts by his supercargoes, making it, says Mr. Townsend Ward, the first zoological garden in Philadelphia. During the occupation of the city by the British, Sir William Howe made his head-quarters in the Cadwalader house, when much of the gallant soldier's good wine was doubtless enjoyed by the red-coated officers. Sir William afterwards removed his head-

---

north of Ireland. In 1838, Miss Montgomery married the Baron Tautphoeus, of Marquardstein Castle, Bavaria, Privy Councillor and Chamberlain to the King. —Burke's " Peerage and Baronetage," 1891.

quarters to a large house on High Street,
above Sixth, which was once the home
of Richard Penn and his wife Polly Masters, to whom the property was given by
her mother as a wedding gift.   Richard
was the most popular of the younger
Penns, and here he and his wife lived in
hospitable old-fashioned style.   While he
had his head-quarters on High Street, General Howe drove Mrs. Israel Pemberton's
handsome coach and pair.   The dignified
owner of the equipage having stipulated
that it should be driven to her house first,
it always stood before her door an hour
before being placed at the disposal of the
British officer.   The house at the corner
of Sixth and High Streets and the one
above it belonged to Robert Morris.   The
latter being considered the most suitable
in the city for the residence of the Chief
Executive, General Washington came here
in 1790.   Mr. Morris occupied the corner
house, where, says Mr. Breck, " he did the
honors of the city by a profuse, incessant,
and elegant hospitality. . . . There was a
luxury in the kitchen, table, parlor, and

street equipage of Mr. and Mrs. Morris that
were to be found nowhere else in America."

To both these houses came all persons
of note who visited Philadelphia from 1790
to 1797. It was in the drawing-room of Mrs.
Robert Morris that the Prince de Broglie
performed his feat of tea-drinking, accepting
one cup of tea after another because they
were offered to him by a lady, as he afterwards explained, adding, "I should be
even now drinking it, if the Ambassador
had not charitably notified me at the
twelfth cup, that I must put my spoon
across it when I wished to finish with this
sort of warm water." Among frequent
guests at the Presidential mansion were
Mr. and Mrs. William Lewis; he a distinguished lawyer and judge under the
first administration, while she, an Irish
beauty, who, from the social life abroad, to
which she had the *entrée* as the daughter
of Sir John Esmonde, of Huntingdon
Castle, Ireland, and as the wife of Richard
Durdin, brought a charm and grace of
manner equal to her beauty into the Re-
publican Court of Mrs. Washington.

On Fourth Street, near Spruce, still stands the home of good Dr. Physick, the magic of whose name, in more senses than one, was enough to cure an ailing mortal, while on Chestnut Street, above Sixth, was the country place of Joshua Carpenter, later the residence of Governor Thomas, Dr. Graeme, the Dickinsons, the Chevalier de la Luzerne, and Judge Tilghman. Recollections of the many notable persons who had at different times occupied this mansion, and perhaps also of the good cheer enjoyed within its halls, suggested Judge Peters's witticism. Passing the old house one day with a friend, who called his attention to the fact that the windows were being taken out previous to tearing down the building, he exclaimed, "Yes, the livers are all gone, and now they are taking out the lights."

In the square below stands our most revered landmark, Independence Hall, precious not only to Philadelphians, but to all Americans and to lovers of liberty everywhere.

The artist and engraver have made us

familiar with the noble and picturesque group of men who signed the Declaration. Here in 1787 was gathered another group, equally noble and quite as picturesque,—soldiers who had taken part in the long war, statesmen, governors, eminent jurists, and men of affairs, in all the bravery of their powdered heads, bag wigs, and velvet suits. Robert Morris walks to the State-House with General Washington, who is his guest. They make a fine appearance on the street, and are met with enthusiastic demonstrations from the people. Mr. Morris is described as a large man, and his portraits show us how kindly and earnest was his face; while the President, in his full suit of black, wearing his dress sword with inimitable grace, tall, commanding, and dignified, is always an imposing figure. There are lines of care upon his face which prove that to have been "the Father of his Country" through eight years of war and five years of unsettled political and social life was no light task.

As they near the House they are met by other delegates,—James Madison, who has "the Virginia plan" safely packed away in his clever head, or perchance the more eloquent Randolph, who is to present it upon the floor; or Rutledge, from South Carolina, or John Dickinson, from nearer home; or it may be that the General bends his tall form to hear what Hamilton has to say as they enter the hall together,—Alexander Hamilton, who at seventeen made a powerful appeal to the New York massmeeting in '74, who was Washington's aide-de-camp in '77, and who now shares with Madison the honor of leading this great Convention.

Here are George Clymer, Elbridge Gerry, Roger Sherman, George Read, and many others who belonged to the Congress of '76, among them James Wilson, the learned Scotchman, who, while declaring that he was not a blind admirer of the Constitution, asserted that, to his mind, "it was the best form of government that had ever been offered to the world," which seems to have been the opinion of Dr. Franklin. The latter, cheerful despite the infirmities of

age, has, as usual, a little story to tell.
This time it is about a French lady who
said to her sister, " I do not know how it
is, my sister, but I meet with nobody but
myself who is always in the right." Just
what this had to do with the Constitution
does not appear, but they all laughed at the
old man's joke, and cheered him heartily
when he declared that he had finally made
up his mind that the carving upon the
back of the Speaker's chair was a " rising
sun," although he had had serious doubts
about it in darker days.

If a painting were to be made of these
statesmen gathered together in the old
hall, it would seem incomplete without
the scholarly and refined face of Francis
Hopkinson. Although not a delegate to
the Convention, he contributed much to
its success by his poems, allegories, and
satires, carrying in that small head, which
John Adams described as not bigger than
a large apple, a vast amount of literary
and legal lore, and withal no end of quips
and quirks and witticisms. But the pen
grows garrulous with reminiscences, from

which we turn to hope that the old building may ever be preserved, an honored
memorial, to which may come in all generations those who would renew their pa-
triotism and strengthen their faith in the
best that belongs to humanity.   A shrine
is this, more sacred than the graves of
heroes, because this is a monument to
principles which are even greater than the
men who fought in their defence.

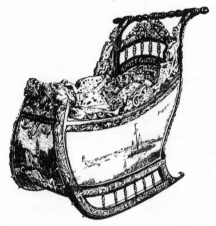

Old Dutch Sledge used in early New York

WEDDINGS AND MERRY-MAKINGS.

" One did commend me to a wife both fair and young
That had French, Spanish, and Italian tongue.
I thanked him kindly and told him I loved none of such,
For I thought one tongue for a wife too much.
What! love ye not the learned?
Yes, as my life.
A learned scholar, but not a learned wife."

SURELY some crabbed bachelor, heavily
fined for remaining in the single state
from which no fair lady would help him

to escape, had composed this venomous doggerel for Ann Wing, aged thirteen, to perpetuate with painstaking stitches. How glad she must have been to turn from it to execute in colored silks the impossible roses and trees that illuminate her beautifully worked sampler!

Hannah Head, who was probably as fond of bright colors as any other Quaker child, inveighs upon her square of canvas against those who

> " Court to be decked in rich attire
>   With gold spread, that others may admire,"

insisting in all colors of the rainbow that

> " They in whose noble heart true virtue dwells,
>   Need not so much adorn their outward shells."

Poor little girls! such words seem strangely unsuited to your years and experience. We can only hope that your lives were brighter than they seem to us as we look back upon them. This hope is encouraged by the fact that Miss Winslow, a regular attendant of the Old South, was allowed to take part in an entertainment where there was dancing, and where the " treat was nuts, raisins, cakes, wine, punch, hot and cold, all in great plenty." The publication of the diary of this Boston school-girl of 1771 throws a more attractive light upon child-life in New England, and leads us to believe that there were others besides Anna Winslow who filled their home letters with descriptions of their innocent pleasures and girlish vanities, even if they, like her, dutifully quoted the text and gave their opinions upon the parson's discourse. After all, girl hearts beat high then as now, and were as quick to respond to the touch of joy or love. Courtship and marriage came so early in those days that the little maids had scarcely finished their samplers and folded them away before they had to take them out again to copy the letters upon the linen for their bridal outfits.

With all the seeming repression of child-life, and the great outward deference shown to the wishes of parents, there seems to have been considerable independence in love-affairs among young women in Colonial

17*

days. Even Betty Sewall refused one husband of her father's choice, and kept another unexceptionable *parti* waiting a year for her answer to his suit; while, from Priscilla Mullins frankly encouraging John Alden to speak for himself, to Phœbe Harrison refusing to give her cherries to any one but the lad for whom they were intended, these gentle creatures seem to have had decided opinions about their partners for life. Phineas Pemberton's "Narrative" tells, in his own words, the quaint story of his love-making:

"Phœbe, with her mother as they were going into Cheshire, called at my master's shop, but I knew them not; she, being then about nine years of age, said to her mother, having got some cherries in her apron, 'I have a mind to give one of these young men some cherries.' Her mother said, 'Then give to both;' one of my fellow apprentices being then by me and on a market day,—I never having seen them before, nor they me, that I know of, and altogether strangers to them. She said, 'No; I will but give to one,' and through the crowd of people that then stood before the counter, she pressed holding out her hand with cherries for me, before I was well aware; and I admired that a child I knew not, should offer me such kindness; but on inquiry remembered I had heard her name, and I retali-

ated her kindness at the same time with a paper of
brown candy.   About two years after that she came
that way again with her mother who came into the shop
but she did not; She only stayed in the street & then
again I remembered her kindness but saw not her face.
About two years after that I went to Bolton to get a
shop, to set up trade there and then saw her again but
remembered little of what before had happened.   After I
was come there and had settled awhile and took notice
of her discreet & modest behavior and features & personage I then was taken with her; She appeared very
lovely in my eye tho' then quite young & because of this
I suppressed my affection for a time.   Other things
in the meanwhile offered on that account to me, but
more & more love increased in me towards her until I
could not conceal it.   I then remembered the beginnings thereof as already mentioned.   Her parents and
friends were very respectful to it but because of her tender years it was still delayed until she was of riper age;
in which time she was often not well, sometimes from
home under the doctor's hands & once at London in
which time many letters passed.

These letters, which were devoutly religious as well as tenderly affectionate, were
followed by the marriage of the Quaker
lovers.   Soon after, being grievously per-
secuted for conscience' sake, Phineas and
Phœbe emigrated to Pennsylvania, where,
as in Massachusetts, the Pemberton name

was soon identified with important work in the Provincial government.

Another Quaker courtship, of much later date, was that of Walter Franklin, of New York, and Hannah Bowne, of Long Island, of which the following record has been preserved in the Franklin family:

" A gentleman riding at his leisure in his chariot [about 1774] passed the door of a thrifty farmer on Long Island. It was a well to do place, but there was nothing to distinguish the house from others in the neighborhood, and he would not have thought of it again, but at the moment a young and beautiful Quaker girl entered the yard to milk the cows that were coming from the pasture. He saw that she was lovely in form and graceful, and scarcely knowing what he did, he reined in his horse and asked who lived there. Without embarrassment, for the speaker was too well dressed and too gentlemanly to excite suspicion, she replied, ' My father, Daniel Bowne, wilt thou not alight and take tea with him?' The invitation was accepted and when the stranger approached the house he introduced himself to Daniel Bowne as Walter Franklin. ' Thou art known to me by reputation,' said Bowne to his visitor, 'and I am glad to see thee.' Then they talked of matters that each thought would interest the other, Franklin not forgetting to praise the cows he had seen in the barnyard, but no mention was made of the maid who milked them. Presently the door opened and the young girl entered to prepare the table and set out the tea things. She was dressed in the simple garb of her people, her hair was carefully smoothed and gathered up into a knot, and a linen kerchief covered her neck and bosom. 'Hannah,' said her father, 'this is friend Walter Franklin of New York.' The girl blushed deeply when she met the ardent look of the stranger, and her embarrassment was none the less when she found that no allusion was made to the previous meeting. Long they sat around the table in that quiet cosy parlor, and when the time to leave had come, the guest bade adieu to the farmer and his daughter promising ere long to visit them again. The promise was faithfully kept, and after three such visits Walter sought and won the hand of Hannah, who, as his wife, rode with him in his chariot to New York. There she presided over his house at the corner of Cherry and Pearl Sts.,* and from what is known of the establishment there were few in the city that surpassed it. Great as was the change in her mode of living, Mrs. Franklin was quite equal to her new position, for she had been taught to cultivate every housewifely virtue, and her mind was stored with learning, as was shown in after years in the rearing of her children."

The daughters of this marriage were gay girls who seem to have left Quakerism far behind them. Two of them married Clintons,—De Witt and his brother George,—

* This handsome old house was the residence of President Washington in 1789.

while their cousin, Sally Franklin, a great belle during the British occupation of New York, married Mr. Robinson, of Newport, and went there to live. The admiration excited in the breasts of French and English officers by the Quaker beauties of Newport has been " sung in song and rehearsed in story," while a portrait of Polly Lawton, in the Redwood Library, smiles down sweet denial of any evil intent in her coquetry.

Among other charmers were the Robinson sisters, who made sad havoc with the hearts of the British officers in Newport. Mrs. Robinson, alarmed by the serious attentions of two of these gentlemen who were quartered in her house, and not being in favor of a foreign alliance, sent off her fascinating daughters upon a visit to their relatives in Narragansett, forbidding their return until the British had left the island. Later the Marquis de Noailles was quartered in the Robinson house,—a pleasant guest, who so fully appreciated the kindness of his hostess that after his return to France he sent Mrs.

Robinson some exquisite Sèvres china, which was accompanied by a charming letter from his lovely young wife.   It is not difficult to believe in the hospitality of this old mansion when we see its great fireplace, where, says tradition, two quarrelsome women cooked for years upon their separate stoves without speaking to each other.

Great simplicity characterized many Colonial weddings, but, yielding to the sweet and wholesome instinct that has always led parents to rejoice and make merry over their children's settling for life, the Colonists gradually surrounded their weddings with more ceremony and gayety.   In families where large fortunes were acquired, a handsome trousseau was usually prepared for the bride.   Before the marriage of his daughter to Nathaniel Sparhawk, Sir William Pepperell wrote to England for an outfit which included

" *Silk* to make a woman a full suit of clothes, the ground to be white padusoy and flowered with all sorts of coulers suitable for a young woman—another of white watered *Taby*, and *Gold Lace* for trimming of it ;

twelve yards of Green Padusoy; thirteen yards of Lace, for a woman's head dress, 2 inches wide, as can be bought for 13 s. per yard; a handsome Fan, with a leather mounting, as good as can be bought for about 20 shillings; 2 pair silk shoes, and cloggs a size bigger than ye shoe."

William Pepperell, the father of Mrs. Sparhawk, seems to have conducted his courtship of Miss Hirst in Oriental fashion, making her presents of gold rings, a large hoop, and other ornaments. "The fair lady," says the family chronicler, "was already wooed by her cousin Moody, a school-master from York, but the modest pretensions of the pedagogue were destined to make no headway against so formidable a rival as the future baronet, who was even then the heir of a fortune, favored with engaging manners and the tact which fashionable life and political eminence confer." So the poor school-master wrote *vale* in the diary in which he had transcribed the charms of his Dulcinea, and the victorious Pepperell led Miss Hirst to the altar.

An old portrait marked " Lady Pepperell and her sister Miss Royal," represent-

ing two demure little maidens of thirteen
and fourteen seated upon a sofa together,
the elder with a humming-bird poised upon
one hand as if to proclaim it an American
painting, attracted the attention of the
writer, and led her to investigate the family
line to learn why there are no Pepperells
in the New England life of to-day. It
transpired that William Pepperell, the
grandson of the victor of Louisburg, who
married Elizabeth Royal, died without
heirs. The name thus became extinct in
America, the family being represented by
Sparhawks, Huttons, Tylers, Snows, and
others. Miriam Tyler, a granddaughter of
Sir William Pepperell, married a certain
Colonel Williams; after her death he married, in turn, a Miss Wells, and for his third
wife a shrewish maid by the name of Dickinson, who treated his children so badly
that they left home and finally joined
the Shakers at Lebanon. Of this marital
experience an epigrammatic friend observed,—

"Colonel Williams married his first wife, Miss
Miriam Tyler, for good sense, and got it; his second

18

wife, Miss Wells, for love and beauty, and had it; and his third wife, Aunt Hannah Dickinson, for good qualities, and got horribly cheated."

A groom who lost his bride upon the steps of the altar was Noahdiah Brainerd. Young Samuel Selden, of Hadlyme, Connecticut, so runs the tale, observing a notice on the door of Chester Meeting-House, stating that Noahdiah Brainerd and Deborah Dudley proposed marriage in that house on the following Lord's day, tore the notice from the door and substituted another, in which the names of Samuel Selden, of Hadlyme, and Deborah Dudley appeared as proposing marriage upon the self-same day. When the wedding-morning arrived, Captain Selden came early to the meeting-house, armed and equipped according to the law, and, observing that his notice was undisturbed, took heart of grace, and when Mr. Joseph Dudley, his wife, and daughter Deborah, appeared, he advanced, addressed the latter affectionately, and led her up the aisle to the minister, who married them according to the solemn forms then obtaining. What the

groom-elect, Noahdiah, was about all this
time we are not informed, but, as the Selden family history records that Samuel
took his bride across the river the same
day, without objection or resistance on
her part, it certainly looked as if the fair
Deborah, like the love of the "young
Lochinvar," was not averse to a change-
ling groom, while the inscription upon
the wedding-ring, still preserved in the
Selden family,—"Beauty is a Fair, but
Virtue is a Precious Jewel,"—shows that
Samuel fully appreciated the various
charms of his daringly won bride. The
strange sequel to this romantic wedding
is that after many years of wedded life
and the birth of several children, upon
the death of her husband, Samuel, Deborah Selden became the wife of her first
lover, Noahdiah Brainerd. The query
very naturally suggests itself, Did she love
him all the time, was she frightened into
marrying her masterful lover, Samuel Selden? and, equally pertinent in those days
of much marrying, Did the defrauded
Noahdiah remain true to his first love all

those years, or did he marry in the interim
and find himself a widower thus oppor-
tunely ?

Somewhat similar to this Puritan love-
story is one preserved in the Esling family
of Philadelphia, although in this latter
tale the bride was the clever strategist, as
appears from the history of the affair.

Mary Magdalen Esling was engaged to
be married to one Thomas Carroll, and
according to the chronicle her wedding-
day was not only fixed, but

"the guests had actually assembled to witness the ceremony; the wedding entertainment was spread, and expense had not been spared; among the rare, and for
those days luxurious adornments of the ample board,
were a number of candelabra containing a curious kind
of candle made by a then well-known artificer, Peter
Field.   These candles were decorated, and by an ingenious process were made to explode in a shower of
beautiful but harmless pyrotechnics.   Everything was
in readiness for the ceremony to begin, the bridal party
had entered.   Suddenly the candles flamed up, to the
astonishment and applause of the company, but when
the excitement had subsided the bride had disappeared.
Taking advantage of the confusion, she had slipped
away from the company, and all arrayed as she was in
her bridal costume, had leaped the rear fence of her
father's garden, and met on the outside one whom she

prized higher than her intended husband, Carroll, a
waiting lover, who bore what was under the circum
stances the very appropriate name of Hauck, since he
had not only swooped down in such an unceremonious
manner on the company, but had also captured her
whom we may poetically designate as the dove, though
practically her conduct bespoke more of the cunning
of the serpent."

Some later weddings that brought with
them a spice of hazard and adventure were
those of Elisha Boudinot * and Colonel
William Duer, which took place in New
Jersey during the Revolution. At the
marriage of Elisha Boudinot and pretty
Kitty Smith, of Elizabethtown, Alexander
Hamilton, who was then Washington's
young aide-de-camp, acted as master of
ceremonies, and, in addition to his other
duties, was obliged to keep a sharp look-
out to prevent a surprise from the enemy.

The marriage of Colonel William Duer
and Lady Kitty Alexander, a daughter of
Lord Stirling, was solemnized at the fine
old Stirling manor-house among the hills

---

* Elisha Boudinot was a brother of Elias Boudinot,
President of Congress, and of Mrs. Richard Stockton,
the poetess.

of Basking Ridge.   To this wedding, says
Emeline G. Pierson, in her sketches of old-
time Jersey weddings, came such aristo-
cratic families of the State as the Bou-
dinots, Stocktons, Hetfields, Kennedys,
Southards, Mortons. Ogdens, Lotts, and
Clarkes.   The manor-house being at the
time the head-quarters of General Greene,
and Washington's camp being at Morris-
town, only eight miles distant, this wedding was something of a military pageant.
Lady Kitty was given away by no less a
personage than the Commander-in-Chief,
while, in addition to the numerous officers
among the guests, the house was surrounded by soldiers, who called for a sight
of the fair bride, and, when she stepped
out upon the lawn, greeted her with ring-
ing cheers and hearty good wishes.

A dignified New York wedding that belongs to a somewhat later period was that
of Mr. Peter Augustus Jay and Miss Mary
R. Clarkson.   The groom was a son of
Chief-Justice Jay and his lovely wife,
Sarah Livingston, the bride a daughter
of General Clarkson.   Mary Clarkson was

evidently a charming girl. Motherless
from early childhood, she was most carefully trained by her father, over whose
home she presided until her marriage.*

After an exchange of letters of congratu-
lation between the Honorable John Jay
and General Clarkson upon the engage-
ment of their children, which was evidently
a source of gratification to both families,
the wedding of Miss Clarkson and Mr.
Jay, whose course of true love ran so
smooth, was solemnized at the Clarkson
house on Pearl Street.

" The company assembled about half-past seven, and
were received in the drawing-room, which was on the

---

* That this exemplary parent was not lacking in a
sense of humor we gather from a letter written to his
daughter Elizabeth, while upon a visit to Mrs. Thomas
Newbold, in Philadelphia. Miss Clarkson had evi
dently enjoyed a serenade from an admirer who was
unknown to her father, as General Clarkson writes,—

" Here, I can tell you, we sleep in peace and quiet-
ness. No one disturbs us at night under our windows,
excepting now and then Aunt Katy's cats, which occa
sionally give us a serenade. As I have informed you
of the party that have annoyed me, I shall expect to be
told in your next who they are that have lately dis
turbed you."

north side of the house on the second floor, its three windows looking out upon Pearl Street. Among the guests, says an eye-witness, were Governor Jay, Miss Anne Brown, the Rutherfurds, Bayards, Le Roys, Van Hornes, Munroes, Wallaces, and others. Bishop Moore arrived a quarter before eight, and at eight the bride, followed by her bridesmaids, entered the room and was received by the groom and his attendants. The bridesmaids were the Misses Ann Jay, Helen Rutherfurd, Anna Maria Clarkson, Cornelia Le Roy, and Susan and Catherine Bayard. The groomsmen were Robert Watts, Jr., John Cox Morris, Dominick Lynch, George Wechman, Benjamin Ledyard, and B. Woolsey Rogers. The bride was dressed in white silk covered with white crape or gauze. Pearls adorned her hair, encircled her neck, and were clasped around her arms. Her maids wore white muslin, made in the style of the Empire, and embroidered in front, and each carried a fan, a present from the bride. 'Drab flesh-colored' small clothes, flesh-colored silk stockings, white vests, and coats varying in color to suit the taste of the wearer made up the attire of the gentlemen, which corresponded with that of the groom. whose coat was of a light color. The ceremony was then performed by the Bishop, and Mrs. Jay received the congratulations of her friends. A great variety of refreshments were then handed round on trays by colored waiters, and in the dining-room below, upon a side table. a collation was spread, of which the elderly people partook. The groomsmen drank a bottle of wine together before separating, and the evening's festivities were over at twelve o'clock. On the next day Mr. and Mrs. Jay went on a visit to Edgerston, on the Passaic, a little above Belleville, the residence of the Hon. John Rutherfurd. On Saturday Mrs. Rutherfurd entertained the bridal party at a breakfast, and on Monday they returned to the city. Mr. Jay received his friends on the mornings of the succeeding Tuesday, Wednesday and Thursday, and Mrs. Jay's receptions were in the evenings of Thursday, Friday and Saturday."

How dignified and leisurely this sounds! Mr. Jay receiving his friends upon three mornings of the week, Mrs. Jay hers in the evening, with no end of breakfasts and dinners between. These prolonged nuptial festivities were undoubtedly a survival of a custom prevalent in some of the Colonies of keeping open house for several days after a wedding. Watson says that weddings in old Philadelphia, even among Friends, were " very expensive and harassing to the wedded." The bride's home was filled with company to dine, the same guests usually staying to tea and supper, while for two days punch was served in great profusion. Kissing the bride and drinking punch seem to have been the leading features of these entertainments. For two days the groom's

friends would call at his house and take
punch, and all would kiss the bride, after
which for a week or more the bride and
groom would give large tea-parties at their
home every evening, the bridesmaids and
groomsmen being always in attendance.
Sometimes a coaching trip was taken to
Lancaster, the bridesmaids and groomsmen still in attendance. The coach would
stop at the General Wayne or the Buck
Tavern, on the Lancaster pike, where
breakfasts would be served to the party.
This more sociable manner of conducting
a wedding trip frequently led to engage-
ments between the attendants, thus pro-
moting and extending happiness. From
Philadelphia and New York longer wedding journeys were occasionally made to
Newport and Providence, many marriages
having taken place between the young
people of these places. Such marriages
were usually among Friends, and were the
results of the Yearly Meetings held in one
or other of the larger towns.

Among the Scotch-Irish in Pennsylvania,
receptions, called " infairs," were held after

the wedding, and were often prolonged through several days. In country places or small towns weddings proved delightful occasions for gathering a neighborhood together. Family coaches or stages brought numbers of guests to the ceremony, and many stayed overnight. There was gossiping, feasting, and punch-drinking galore for the older people, and for the young all the pleasant exchange of smiles and glances and gay nothings that would eventually lead to other weddings in the same circle.

A Harrisburg antiquary says of old-time weddings,—

"They were not the brief, soulless affairs of to-day Guests sometimes arrived before breakfast and remained until the 'wee sma' hours' of night, and not unfrequently Aurora herself escorted them home. The hours of daylight were spent in plays full of life and spirit, such as 'Shove the Brogan,' 'The Meat's a-Burning,' etc., interspersed with breathing spells for refreshments, when wit and humor had free scope, and such out-door sports as 'Prisoner's Base' and 'Jump the Bullies.' (The latter was purely a masculine game which offered the 'young fellows' an excellent opportunity to display their agility.) And when night let fall her sable curtain, the halls resounded with instrumental music and dancing and the voice of song."

Although we do not hear as much of "bride stealing" in the Middle Colonies as in New England, the groom was not allowed to quit the ranks of the single without a parting salute from his companions. A custom prevailed in Southern Pennsylvania, and among the Scotch-Irish in Virginia, of barring the progress of the coach of the newly married pair by ropes or other obstacles, which were not removed until the groom paid toll in the form of a bottle of wine or of drinks to his persecutors. These and other customs, which seem to us so rude, do not appear to have seriously interfered with matrimony, and the brides were as fair and as modest as those of to-day, while the grooms were equally handsome, and how much more picturesque!

An old Philadelphian who has lived long enough to recall the early years of this century describes a handsome, imposing house on High Street, between

Seventh and Eighth, and tells of the pleasure she found in looking from the windows of her Quaker home opposite upon the gay doings in this more worldly mansion. Miss Beck, the young lady of the house, has remained a lovely picture in her memory, and she says that she can see her now as she used to come down the marble steps in her dainty slippers with their ribbons crossed and tied around her trim ankles, her long, flowing crape scarf about her shoulders, her high scoop hat with its many feathers and large veil gracefully festooned over its brim, the clustering curls upon her forehead, and her beautiful, bright face beneath. To see her enter her carriage was always a delight; but the day of days in the memory of this imaginative child was when the lady whom she admired so much came down the steps as a bride in her travelling-dress of rich silk, attended by the groom, who was brave in satin, velvet, and shining buckles, while her two brothers walked behind her, each holding in a leash his favorite greyhound. When the steps of the great black chariot

with its yellow wheels were let down and
the bride stepped in and the groom took
his place beside her, the moment was in-
tense, thrilling; the last act in the drama
of love. Are there any such weddings
now? Are there any brides like those
who to the children living opposite were
veritable fairy princesses from Andersen's
tales?

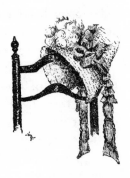

The last of Group of Buildings of the
Friends' Almshouse - Philadelphia

LEGEND AND ROMANCE.

THE search after the truth concerning a
personage or a place mentioned in fiction
may be as fruitless in practical results as
the pursuit of the pot of gold at the end
of the rainbow; yet how fascinating is
such a quest, presupposing, as it does, the
power of those who enter upon it to create
for themselves a world of fancy, a fool's
paradise, or whatever you may choose to
call it, which is in itself a rare and delight-

ful faculty! That this power has not been destroyed by the serious business of living in the nineteenth century appears from the fact that hundreds of pilgrims still follow Dickens through the London haunts of his characters, or visit old Salem and wander through its historic streets in search of the " House of the Seven Gables." This latter quest is carried on with fresh interest every year, although Mr. Hawthorne has carefully explained in the preface to his romance that his characters " have a great deal more to do with the clouds overhead than with any portion of the actual soil of the County of Essex," and that " he trusts not to be considered as unpardonably offending by laying out a street that infringes upon nobody's private rights, and appropriating a lot of land which has no visible owner, and building a house of materials long in use for constructing castles in the air."

An illustration of this trait of humanity, for which no appropriate name suggests itself, is afforded by the interest shown within a few years in a controversy re-

garding the Philadelphia meeting-place of
the Acadian lovers in " Evangeline." Mr.
Longfellow described the almshouse as it
appeared in the plague-stricken town in
1793. In view of the fact that the poet
visited Philadelphia thirty years after the
events narrated, and doubtless saw the
two almshouses then standing, it is not
improbable that he so confused them in
his own mind that he was able to form an
harmonious picture from the more salient
features of the two. This explanation
would not, however, satisfy the insatiate
delver after truth. Mr. Frank A. Burr
opened the discussion by stating authoritatively that the scene of the meeting of Evangeline and Gabriel was the
almshouse on Spruce Street, between
Tenth and Eleventh, and their burial-
place the yard of old Christ Church,
where he speaks of visiting the grave of
the lovers and pushing aside the ivy that
had grown over their imaginary tombstone
A local antiquary, Mr. Esling, who had
given much attention to the subject in connection with the Church of St. Joseph's,

stepped in promptly and furnished excellent arguments in favor of the Friends' Almshouse on Willing's Alley as the place where the lovers met, quoting a letter from Mr. Longfellow himself, in which, after thanking Mr. Esling for some photographs taken just before the building was destroyed, he says,—*

"I cannot quite make out from the photographs whether this is the place I had in mind when writing the last scene of the poem. I only remember brick walls, an enclosure, and large trees; a building I saw many years ago when walking the streets of your city, and whose memory came back to me as I wrote. Be this as it may, I thank you cordially for your kindness and highly appreciate this act of good will on your part. Is there not still standing in Philadelphia, in some remote street, an almshouse or hospital with brick walls and a garden with trees?

"If so, I may possibly see once more the very place I had in memory. If not, then I shall think that this

* The last buildings of the Friends' Almshouse were not removed until the spring of 1876. Another institution that has been brought into the controversy is the Friends' "bettering-house," near Second and Pine Streets. This is out of the question, however, as it was not used as an almshouse or hospital after 1767, and could not have been visited as such by Mr. Longfellow in 1824.

demolished cottage was a part of the place described in the last scene of the poem."

The almshouse on Spruce Street and the quaint little building on Walnut Place having been destroyed prior to Mr. Longfellow's visit to Philadelphia in 1876, the only individual who could speak authoritatively upon the subject was unable to decide the matter. Consequently, the readers of the poem are perfectly free to form their own opinions and locate for themselves the pathetic scene when Evangeline, after her long quest in search of her lover, enters the hospital ward with flowers in her hands, the bloom of the morning in her face, to see Gabriel lying there, " motionless, senseless, dying." The Quaker Almshouse, covered with ivy and trumpet-flowers, and surrounded by its beds of herbs and flowers, certainly furnished a more picturesque setting for the last and most dramatic scene in the poem than did the Spruce Street building; yet Mr. Longfellow's description seems to apply better to the more spacious grounds of the latter, as he speaks of entering through the gates, of wandering through the grounds and sitting under the large trees with the poor, listening to their stories of the life within. These expressions were used in after-years in speaking to Mr. Burr of his visit to Philadelphia in 1824, when the almshouse and its surroundings so impressed themselves upon his mind that they recurred to him later when he wrote his poem, and led him to place the final scene

" In that delightful land which is washed by the Delaware's waters."

Dr. Charles K. Mills, in his history of the Philadelphia Almshouse, says that there is no question in his mind that this was the spot visited by Mr. Longfellow in 1824.

" As it was in 1755 that the French Acadians of Grand Pré—nineteen hundred peaceful, happy souls—were dispossessed of their homes and began their wanderings, the event idealized by the poet can probably be referred to the epidemic of yellow fever in 1793, and to the almshouse building at Tenth and Spruce Streets, first occupied in 1767."

As there is no proof to bring forward,

the poet's mind naturally being much more
intent upon the romantic story of the Acadians and the broader outlines of his poem
than upon definite localities, the surroundings of the last scene in the drama are still
left in the nebulous region of uncertainty,
which is the most appropriate setting for a
romance.   With regard to the burial-place
of the lovers there can be no question, for,
as Mr. Esling clearly demonstrates, the
only spot that answers to Mr. Longfellow's
description is "the little church down the
alley."

"Side by side, in their nameless grave, the lovers are
      sleeping.
   Under the humble walls of the little Catholic church-
      yard,
   In the heart of the city, they lie."

So in the Catholic church of St. Joseph's,
set like a mosaic in the midst of dingy
alleys and high buildings, we leave the dear,
constant old lovers to sleep their last sleep.
Little did they dream that their obscure
love-story would lead so many clever people to talk about them, nor would it, had
   p

not the hand of the poet touched it with the magic of his genius.

Two heroines who lived, not in the misty realm of fiction, but in the clear, bright light of day, were Flora Macdonald and Rebecca Gratz. The former, from the moment that she appears upon the pages of history with her heroic offer of service—"Since I am to die, and can die but once, I am perfectly willing to put my life in jeopardy to save his Royal Highness"—to the hour of her death, when she was still loyal to the memory of Prince Charlie, presents a character of singular frankness, courage, and devotion. After the escape of the prince who seemed so unworthy of the lives risked in his defence, Flora Macdonald was taken prisoner and carried to London. When it transpired that the Scotch maiden was not a Jacobite, but simply a devoted child of monarchy, she was courted and fêted by the nobility, and even granted an audience by George II. "How dared you to succor the enemy of my crown and kingdom?" was the disconcerting query of the king, to which

Flora replied, without embarrassment, " It was no more than I would have done for your Majesty, had you been in like situation."

During her sojourn in London, where her life was a round of festivities, Flora's portrait was painted for Commodore Smith, whose sloop had conveyed her to the metropolis as a prisoner. Later she left London in a coach-and-four, in company with Malcolm Macleod, a fellow-conspirator, and five years after married one of her own clansmen, Allan Macdonald, the young Laird of Kingsburgh, whose mother had aided in the escape of the prince. Flora became mistress of the mansion in which Charles Edward had passed his first night on the Isle of Skye. Here, in 1773, Mrs. Macdonald entertained Dr. Johnson and Mr. Boswell, the Highland hostess being described by the latter as " a little woman, of a genteel appearance and uncommonly mild and well-bred." Later, Mr. Boswell records that he slept at the Macdonalds' in the same room with Dr. Johnson, and had the pleasure of seeing the great lexicographer ensconced in the bed in which Prince Charles Edward lay after the battle of Culloden, when thirty thousand pounds were offered as a reward for apprehending him. "To see Dr. Samuel Johnson lying in that bed in the Isle of Skye, in the house of Miss Flora Macdonald (for so I shall call her), struck me with such a group of ideas as it is not easy for words to describe, as they passed through my mind. He [Dr. Johnson] smiled and said, ' I have no ambitious thoughts in it.' " At breakfast the next morning Mrs. Macdonald related her adventures, to the great satisfaction of Dr. Johnson, and of Mr. Boswell, who of course made full notes of the conversation.

In 1774 the Macdonalds sailed from Cambelton, Kintyre, for Wilmington, North Carolina. Hither Flora's fame had preceded her and she was received with open arms. A grand ball was given in her honor in Wilmington, and upon her approach to Cross Creek (now Fayetteville) she was greeted with strains of the pibroch and the martial airs of her native land.

For some time she remained among her friends at Cross Creek, and the site of her home is still shown, although the house is now in ruins. Later the Macdonalds removed to Cameron's Hill in Cumberland County, and afterwards to Anson County.

During the early years of the Revolution Mrs. Macdonald and her family—many of the clan having come to America—exerted great influence over the Highlanders in North Carolina. This influence was naturally in favor of the crown, and was of great service to Martin, the Tory governor of the State. At the battle of Moore's Creek, in February, 1776, a number of loyalists led by Donald Macdonald were defeated and routed. After the battle the victorious Americans found General Macdonald sitting alone on a stump near his tent, waving in the air the parchment scroll containing his commission, which he delivered into their hands. Over eight hundred common soldiers were made prisoners, disarmed, and discharged, while a number of officers were taken to the jail in Halifax. Among these were Allan Mac-

donald, the husband of Flora, and one
or more of her sons. Although she had
taken no active part in the conflict, she exerted a powerful influence over her clansmen, urging them forward to fight for their
King. Allan Macdonald, " on consideration of his candor and his being in a low
state of health," was released on parole,
and he and his wife and daughter returned
to Scotland either in 1779, or in 1782, ac-
counts varying as to the date. The sloop
in which the Macdonalds embarked upon
their homeward voyage was pursued by a
French vessel, and was in imminent danger
of capture, when Flora ascended the
quarter-deck, and, nothing daunted, encouraged the men to renewed efforts. The
sight of this woman, so courageous in the
face of danger and suffering, raised the
spirits of the crew, and the French were
finally beaten and Flora safely landed
upon her native soil, where she passed
the remainder of her days. She is said
to have remarked more than once, with
charming candor and good humor, " I
have hazarded my life both for the house

of Stuart and the house of Hanover, and I do not see that I am a great gainer by it."

A heroine of eminence associated with the land of Flora Macdonald, although she never set foot upon its picturesque shores, was Rebecca Gratz, of Philadelphia. Men and women still in the prime of life can recall the face and form of an elderly woman, slight and elegant, with gray curls and dark eyes, who was pointed out to them, in their childhood, as the heroine of " Ivanhoe." This was a marvel and a wonder past understanding, and ever after, as Miss Gratz passed along the street, she was looked upon by the children who had heard this tale with a feeling of awe and reverence, as one who had come fresh and fair from the land of romance. Henceforth, in their minds, the face and figure of Rebecca Gratz stood forth from the enchanting background of barbaric splendor and chivalric sentiment against which the novelist has placed the beautiful Jewess, they never doubting that she had passed through the exciting scenes of the tournament at Ashby, the lonely castle of Front-de-Bœuf, and even the final rescue from a violent death by the " Disinherited Knight."

Long after these early impressions were made, it was explained how this Philadelphia woman had come to be the heroine of " Ivanhoe." Washington Irving was a friend of the Gratz family, and often visited them in their old mansion, where he was sure of finding a warm welcome and a room to " roost in," as he expressed it. In addition to this family friendship, Rebecca Gratz was the intimate friend of Matilda Hoffman, of New York, to whom Washington Irving was engaged and to whom he was devotedly attached. The sad story of that early love and loss is well known. Matilda Hoffman, fair and lovely, worthy such a heart as that of Irving, fell into a rapid decline and died at eighteen, leaving what the world seldom sees,—an absolutely inconsolable lover. Rebecca Gratz nursed her friend through her last illness and held her in her arms when she died. After the death of Matilda Hoffman, the two survivors were drawn together in a friendship that lasted as long as they both lived.

Miss Gratz is described in her youth as a woman of distinguished beauty. Her eyes were large and dark, her figure graceful, and her manners winning and attractive. In addition to these charms, she was a woman of more than ordinary cultivation and force of character.

During Washington Irving's visit to Great Britain in 1817 he met most of the *literati* of that brilliant period, among them the poet Campbell, who, well aware of Walter Scott's high estimate of Irving's genius, gave him a letter of introduction to the Northern minstrel. Irving, in one of his letters, tells of the informal and cordial reception given him by the poet, who came limping down to the gate to meet him and made him spend several days at Abbotsford, during which time Scott, most delightful of cicerones, visited with him Dryburgh Abbey, and pointed out to him from a mountain-top the Braes of Yarrow Ettrick's stream winding down to throw itself into Tweed, and many another famous spot. After the day's wanderings they read and talked together, and it was

20*

probably upon one of these evenings at
Abbotsford that the older poet drew Irving
to speak of his friends at home, and among
them of Rebecca Gratz. He described
her wonderful beauty, related the story of
her firm adherence to her religious faith
under the most trying circumstances, and
particularly illustrated her loveliness of
character and zealous philanthropy. Scott,
who was deeply interested and impressed,
conceived the plan of embodying in a
romance the noble character and sentiments of this high-souled Jewess. He
was then at work upon " Rob Roy," but
was already revolving in his active mind
the plot of " Ivanhoe," and was desirous
of introducing a Jewish female character
into the story.

We can readily understand how Scott's
imagination was fired by Irving's glowing
description of his beautiful and gifted friend,
and why it is that " Rebecca the Jewess"
stands out for all time as one of the finest
creations of that master-hand. Lockhart
tells us that Scott received letters from
some of the readers of " Ivanhoe " cen-

suring him for bestowing the hand of
Rowena, rather than that of Rebecca, upon
the brave knight of Ivanhoe, showing that
there was in this character "that touch
of nature that makes the whole world
kin." Laidlaw, to whom a large portion
of "Ivanhoe" was dictated, relates that
he became so interested in the story of
Rebecca that he exclaimed as he wrote,
"That is fine, Mr. Scott! Get on! get
on!" To which the author, well pleased,
replied, "Ay, Willie; but recollect I have
to make the story. I shall make something of my Rebecca." "Ivanhoe"
was published in December, 1819, and Sir
Walter sent a copy to Irving and a letter
accompanying it, in which he said, "How
do you like your Rebecca? Does the
Rebecca I have pictured compare with
the pattern given?"

Miss Gratz knew the source of the character of Rebecca, but, "shrinking as she
did from any publicity, would seldom acknowledge the fact, and, when pressed upon
the subject, would deftly evade it by a
change of topic." Belonging to a family

of influence and culture, she naturally met
men of superior position and abilities.
Among those who surrounded her it is
said that there was one man who loved
Rebecca Gratz, who was worthy of her, and
who gained her affection.   The difference
in religious belief, however, proved an in-
surmountable barrier to a union, this latter-
day heroine being as loyal to the faith of
her fathers as was Scott's Rebecca.   Greatly
admired by a large circle of friends in
Philadelphia, at Saratoga Springs, where
she spent her summers, and at her brother's
home in Kentucky where Henry Clay
paid her marked attention, Miss Gratz
seems to have put aside all thoughts of
love and marriage, and to have dedicated
her best energies to works of benevolence
and philanthropy.   There was, says her
biographer, Gratz Van Rensselaer, scarce
a charitable institution of the day in her
native city that did not have the name of
Rebecca Gratz inscribed upon its records
as an active officer or as an adviser and
benefactress, Gentiles as well as Jews being
the recipients of her unfailing kindness

and sympathy. In view of this long life
of devoted service for humanity of one
who, in her youth, seemed fitted pre-emi-
nently for a brilliant social career, we are
reminded of the words of Rebecca in her
final interview with Wilfred's bride :

"Among our own people, since the time of Abraham
downwards, have been women who have devoted their
thoughts to Heaven and their actions to works of kindness to men, tending the sick, feeding the hungry, and
relieving the distressed. Among these will Rebecca be
numbered."

It seems as if the novelist had not only
portrayed the character of Rebecca Gratz
in that of his favorite heroine, but had also
forecast the future of her prototype in these
words of " Rebecca the Jewess."

INDEX.

239

THE END.